Literary Criticism of the Old Testament

by
Norman C. Habel

Fortress Press
Philadelphia

Biblical quotations from the Revised Standard Version of the Bible, copyrighted 1946, 1952, © 1971, 1973 by the Division of Christian Education of the National Council of the Churches of Christ in the U.S.A., are used by permission.

Copyright © 1971 by Fortress Press

Library of Congress Catalog Card Number 78-157548
ISBN 0-8006-0176-9

Second printing 1973
Third printing 1975
Fourth printing 1977
Fifth printing 1979

Library of Congress Catalog Card Number 78-157548
ISBN 0-8006-0176-9

8308L79   Printed in the United States of America   1-176

Editor's Foreword

The production of the Hebrew Bible was a long and complicated process. In all its stages, from beginning to end, it lasted well over a thousand years; and each attempt to describe it discloses more of its complexity.

Despite many changes in special aims and tasks, modern scholarship has persisted with great constancy in its intention of telling the story of how the Bible came to be. Its orientation has been historical and its efforts to describe the contents of the Old Testament and their history have developed three clearly distinguishable methods of study: literary criticism, form criticism, and tradition criticism. Each one of these is really a discipline in its own right. All are interested in the whole story; but each one constitutes a sort of crosscut attempt at giving its account of the whole. And so each one has developed its own techniques and methods of analysis, appropriate to the phenomena on which it concentrates.

Since they "dug in" at very different points in the complex legacy, and since they developed methods of scientific work as distinctive as their special tasks, these three disciplines sometimes give the impression of being arrayed against each other in mutually exclusive fashion. That is not the case; they are interrelated. All three want to contribute to the telling of one story. Their interrelationship is organic and logical. Each discipline lives off the questions that have baffled the other two. Since none of the three is able to ask or deal with all of the questions that must be asked and dealt with to tell the story of the making of the Old Testament, and since all want to tell that story, their relationships are complementary. It is thus fitting that these three small volumes, corresponding to the three disciplines of modern criticism, should appear under a single title, "Guides to Biblical Scholarship."

Literary criticism was the first on the scene. At the outset it was a special variation of textual study. Concentrating on the Book of Genesis, Astruc discovered a literary pattern related to the variant use of the divine names which led him to conclude that, in dealing with the era of the patriarchs, Moses had made use of more than one document or "source" in producing the first book of the Bible. There was an Elo-

iii

hist source and a Yahwist one. The variant use of the divine names came to an end in the third chapter of Exodus. However, using the characteristics of the sources discovered by means of it as criteria, scholars soon extended documentary source study into the entire Pentateuch, and to the Book of Isaiah!

With the movement that carries the name of Wellhausen, literary criticism took a new turn; having focused on the discovery of documentary sources and the marks of their identification, it now began to ask about the setting and motivation that had originally prompted the production of these separate units. One of the incidental by-products of this development was that literary criticism now often carried the popular name of "historical criticism," or "higher criticism," to differentiate it from textual criticism which was "lower!" Of more profound significance for our understanding of the meaning of the whole story was the fact that this movement assumed that the production of Scripture was conditioned historically not only by the fact that it had combined documents with a prior history of their own, but also that wider movements in human life had influenced their contents. Implicit questions about revelation and the inspiration of Scripture were made more pressing.

Historical criticism complicated the questions about documentary sources raised by the earlier phase of literary criticism; but it could not deal with them. For example, though there was general agreement that the Pentateuch combined four sources, there was no unanimity about precisely what belonged to each of these. More serious still were the disagreements about the antecedent history of each of the four. Did each combine two or more separate units? And could one detect the hand of the redactor who had combined them? Or was each of the four strands a single unit that had gone through several stages of annotation and editing? And how large a role had been played by the final redactor(s) who had given the Pentateuch or the Book of Isaiah their present forms? The riddles were growing in number and the frustration they produced called for a new beginning. It was in this context that form criticism arose.

In his famous essay, "The Problem of the Hexateuch," written in the thirties, G. von Rad tells how the old methods of literary criticism failed to deal with his questions. In his frustration the rubrics for the presentation of the offering of first fruits caught his attention. This text (Deuteronomy 26:1–11) was one of the relatively few in which the prescriptions for what is to be done in a situation are combined with the words to be recited. It was the form of the recital—an enumeration of the acts of God in Israel's history—that von Rad found most important; he called it a *Credo*, and he proceeded to build his interpretation of all of Israel's traditions around this form. Gunkel and Mowinckel were pioneers in form criticism who preceded von Rad; but what is striking about the case of von Rad is how the limitations of literary criticism landed him in form criticism.

Form criticism concentrates on primary categories of form rather than on documents: the hymn, the blessing, the legend, the lament, and many, many more. That is its most original contribution. It combines this concentration with the historical interest in setting and function first stressed by the historical critics of Wellhausen's day. Who used a given form? in what context? and for what purposes? Form criticism depends greatly on the results of research in such areas as cult and liturgy, social psychology, and anthropology, for the meaning of a given unit depends as much on its function in the life of the community as on the positive contents of its form. Indeed, many form critics would insist that this *Sitz im Leben* is of far greater importance than contents for our understanding; and all would probably agree that it is indispensable.

The internal tensions and bifurcations in the practice of form criticism parallel those we have noted in literary criticism. There a study of the documents themselves competed with an interest in describing the social and political scene in which they were written. Here the analysis of the forms and the exposition of their contents is crowded by a desire to describe the character and significance of the ceremonial that originally developed them. This distinction is classically illustrated by two pioneers in the form critical movement, Hermann Gunkel and his pupil, Sigmund Mowinckel. Both concentrated most of their work on the Book of Psalms. Gunkel assumed psalms were essentially personal and private compositions, even when produced to express a public or communal mood. Though he recognized that their forms were shaped in ancient cultic settings, he was less preoccupied with those settings and their role than with the thought of the authors of psalms. Mowinckel reversed the focus. He became a historian of religion and cult, assuming that psalms had been written for the sake of their role in the actual ceremonial of worship rather than simply for the sake of expressing the experience of an individual author. Mowinckel himself expressed the distinction in the original Norwegian title of his great work, *The Psalms in Israel's Worship*. He called it *Offersang og Sangoffer*, which can be translated "Song of sacrifice and Sacrifice of song." Gunkel had stressed the latter; the song was the thing. Mowinckel emphasized the former; the liturgy which the song was to serve.

Literary criticism dealt with units of the Bible, and with the historical settings in which the writing occurred. Form criticism deals with an earlier preliterary phase of the story. At that stage Israel made its public witness to its understanding of itself in its relation to God in a wide variety of fixed forms suited to oral communication: blessings, oaths, hymns, legends, commandments, and many, many more. Eventually the forms became imbedded in Israel's literature. The process of self-definition which was so productive of what eventually became literary forms, took place in an almost endless variety of circumstances in relation to the family, the temple, the school, the courts, the realm of the state and diplomacy, commerce and trade—to name some of the primary orbits. Sometimes a specific act of this endless process of self-definition involved only a single Israelite. In other instances many persons or recognized groups participated in this process. Very often, too, the whole community of Israel expressed itself in these specific occasions that gave shape to and confirmed the use of particular forms.

Form criticism presupposes that, however unwittingly, all Israelites over many centuries contributed to the making of the Bible; that it was simply a result of their having had a communal existence as Israelites. The interest and intention of form criticism is analytical; it concentrates on detailed aspects of the common life and on the specific forms nurtured by them. There is an interest in the pristine structure of such forms which views all subsequent elaboration or mixing of forms in larger units as a sort of secondary development. There is less interest in telling the story of the making of the Bible as a whole than in describing separately a great number of "scenes" that are finally to be absorbed by that story. Form criticism does not really answer the questions of literary criticism about the editing and combining of documentary units. It puts them in parentheses while going behind them to an earlier stage in the process. There it discloses scenes in the history of the making of the Bible hitherto unknown, scenes in which the practices of common life rather than writing are conspicuous. Thus, for the time being, the unanswered questions left by literary criticism are relativized in their importance, and left untouched. But eventually they reassert themselves, for analysis of primary scenes alone is not capable of telling the story.

Tradition criticism—in New Testament studies the preferred term is "redaction criticism"—responds to a new urge to tell the whole story. Its intentions are synthetic and presuppose the analytic work of both literary and form criticism. Since it follows in the wake of both, it assumes that both oral and written continuities play a role in the shaping of the traditions that finally culminated in Scripture. Individual historians of tradition will vary with respect to the emphasis they place upon one or the other. A comparison of the work of Martin Noth with that of Ivan Engnell illustrates this variation rather well. More significant, perhaps, than their differences in approach and method—or in results—is the fact that both presuppose and use the results of the efforts of literary and form criticism. The proportional significance assigned to oral and written means of transmission, respectively, is a minor matter compared to the common recognition that the whole community, in all expressions of its existence, participated in giving shape to the tradition and in handing it on, generation after generation.

Form criticism concentrates on primary forms—on the beginnings of the shaping of the traditions that finally result in the Old Testament. Redaction criticism, as distinct from tradition history, deals with the very last stages of the editing that presents Scripture in its fixed or final form. Tradition criticism is interested in all the stages that lie in between form and redaction criticism, the history of a tradition which, in the Old Testament, spans more than a millennium. In New Testament studies, which deal in a time span less than a tenth as long, there is an understandable tendency to conflate the study of tradition with that of the final process of editing. The situation is very different with respect to the Old Testament where the history of tradition contains so many facets and stages, all of which can by no means be described as "redactional." Form criticism helps to make us aware of that.

Literary criticism tried to tell the story of the making of the Bible as a story of writing and editing. At the crest of its influence it had asked a great many questions about the history of this process which it found unanswerable on the basis of literary presuppositions alone. Form criticism introduced the presupposition that the making and transmission of the contents of the Bible had an oral as well as a written side to it. This has given tradition critics the sort of freedom and flexibility which literary criticism lacked, and from the lack of which it suffered. This freedom has resulted in promising new essays. As an example, one may refer to Martin Noth's proposal. He suggests that there was a Deuteronomic Historian, a single personality, who made use of all of the older materials contained in that part of the Old Testament that begins with Deuteronomy and ends with 2 Kings. This proposal was Noth's way of getting across some quite specific and personal notions about the meaning of Israel's history. Making this proposal depends on the sort of awareness of openness and freedom made possible by form criticism. Literary criticism had always contemplated the tying together of the material in these books as a process carried on by a series of "Deuteronomic editors," conforming to the notion that the growth of tradition was by a process of writing, only. Noth's imagination and skill as a historian of tradition who presupposes a more open situation because of the oral character of much in the tradition enable him to endow this large section of the Old Testament with a freshness, a pointed clarity, and a unity such as it never had before.

It becomes increasingly clear that the three disciplines featured in this series are interdependent, as well as distinct. They all want to tell the same story; and they need each other's help in doing so. And they can help each other because, as we said at the outset, the orientation of all three is historical.

The historicality of the Bible, that is, the conditioned character of its contents, a conditioned-ness which makes them dependent upon all kinds of human limitations and situations in precisely the same way as the legacies of all sorts of historical traditions, is an assumption of modern criticism throughout. That assumption makes it modern. At the outset the assumption was held very tentatively, even fearfully, and in relatively circumscribed fashion. It asserted itself in the face of venerable traditions of dogma and confessional authority that equated the form of the contents of Scripture, its verbal conceptualizations, with the divine absolute. But the assumptions so gingerly held at the outset were to vindicate their tenability and importance in the process. The Bible is a far more historical book than the pioneers of historical criticism ever dreamed; and we are aware of this precisely because what they began continued: from literary criticism, to form criticism, to tradition criticism. In one way or another, over a period of more than a thousand years, the whole cultural setting of the ancient world of the Near East and every Israelite in all those centuries had some sort of a hand in the making of the Bible.

Needless to say, the impact of these developments on theology has been tremendous and continues as a powerful influence today. The word of God in relation to Scripture, as well as in relation to the church and the world, is being redefined and conceptualized in dynamic, fresh ways today because of the theological implications of modern criticism. Criticism set out to tell the story of the Bible. It did not intend to deal with theology, let alone launch new movements in theology. Nevertheless, however unintentionally, it did both.

J. Coert Rylaarsdam

Contents

I
Introducing Literary Criticism

THE DISCIPLINE OF LITERARY CRITICISM

The Old Testament is a literary masterpiece. As such it invites us to appreciate its literary features as we interpret its unique content. The student today has numerous tools at his disposal for accomplishing this task. In one respect, however, he may be at a disadvantage. Many writers who provide guidelines for Old Testament study base their work on the "assured results of literary criticism." Others imply that the discipline of literary criticism has been superseded by more recent disciplines such as form criticism and redaction criticism. Thus Old Testament literary criticism in the traditional sense is either assumed or ignored. It is rarely defined, demonstrated, or pursued as a vital discipline. Faced with this dilemma the critical student is driven to reexamine the validity of Old Testament literary criticism for himself. He needs to ask again the questions posed by former Old Testament literary critics. He needs to observe anew the literary critical process at work on specific Old Testament texts. He needs to follow this critical procedure afresh, step-by-step from the beginning. But he needs to undertake this task fully aware of how more recent disciplines modify and complement the work of the literary critic. This brief volume is designed to assist the student in answering these needs.

What then is Old Testament literary criticism in the traditional sense? How have past literary critics approached the biblical text? We could answer these questions with a comprehensive survey of the history of Old Testament literary criticism.[1] Or we could compare the principles of Old Testament literary criticism with those of disciplines bearing the

---

1. Adequate surveys of the history of biblical criticism can be found in many Old Testament Introductions and Bible Dictionaries. See especially, K. Grobel, "Biblical Criticism" and S. J. De Vries, "History of Biblical Criticism" in *Interpreter's Dictionary of the Bible*, ed. G. A. Buttrick (Nashville: Abingdon Press, 1962); H. E. Hahn, *The Old Testament in Modern Research* (Philadelphia: Fortress Press, 1966); Hans-Joachim Kraus, *Geschichte der historisch-kritischen Erforschung des Alten Testaments*, 2nd ed. (Neukirchen, 1969); E. Kraeling, *The Old Testament since the Reformation* (New York: Harper, 1955).

same name in other literary fields.[2] Instead, we have chosen a direct textual approach. We invite you to consider the Sinai episode of Exodus 24. And we ask you to note the kind of questions an Old Testament critic poses as he scrutinizes this text. What is the literary plan or structure of this section? Is the passage a literary whole? Can certain literary units be isolated within the chapter? The critic will notice that one major focus of Exodus 24 is God's advent on Mount Sinai. But his questions will lead him to see that at three different points in the account Moses is summoned by God to ascend the mountain. After each summons Moses' ascent is reported. The following extracts from Exodus 24 illustrate this piece of evidence.

A. And he (God) said to Moses, "*Come up to Yahweh*, you and Aaron, Nadab and Abihu and the seventy elders" (v. 1) . . . *So Moses went up* with Aaron, Nadab and Abihu and the seventy elders of Israel, and they saw the God of Israel; and there was under his feet as it were a pavement of sapphire stone, like the very heaven for clearness; and he did not lay his hand on the chief men of the people of Israel; they beheld God and ate and drank (vv.9–11).

B. And Yahweh said to Moses, "*Come up to me* on the mountain and wait there; and I will give you the tables of stone, with the law and the commandment, which I have written for their instruction." So Moses rose with his servant Joshua, and Moses went up into the mountain of God. And he said to the elders, "Tarry here for us until we come to you again. And behold, Aaron and Hur are with you; whoever has a cause let him go to them." *Then Moses went up* on the mountain (vv. 12–15a).

C. Then the cloud covered the mountain. The glory of Yahweh settled on Mount Sinai, and the cloud covered it six days; and on the seventh day *he called to Moses* out of the midst of the cloud. Now the appearance of the glory of the Lord was like a devouring fire on the mountain in the sight of all the people of Israel. And Moses entered the cloud and *went up* on the mountain (vv. 15b–18a).

This division suggests the possibility of three distinct literary units or three stages of literary composition. Do we have one literary artist involved or three? Are the three summons to ascend Sinai separate introductions by three different writers? The critic returns to the text. He compares these three pieces of Exodus 24 for internal connections or inconsistencies of thought. As he does so he is met with the prob-

2. Literary criticism, in a general way, can mean any kind of critical appreciation of literature. Recently literary criticism has also been associated with hermeneutical discussions. William Beardslee's treatment of *Literary Criticism in the New Testament* in the companion New Testament series embraces this aspect in his definition of the discipline.

lem of who accompanies Moses to the top of Sinai. In the first unit Moses, Aaron, Nadab, Abihu, and the seventy elders ascend Sinai together. In the second Moses travels with Joshua, while Aaron, Hur, and the elders remain behind. In the third unit Moses seems to be alone on the mountain.

This kind of evidence may suggest the work of several writers speaking from divergent perspectives. And so the critic asks a further question. Do the differences of viewpoint in these three sections of Exodus 24 go even deeper? Does each unit reflect a distinctive theological concern? The first segment (vv. 1–11) focuses upon the covenant relationship between Israel and its God. That relationship is viewed in the context of a covenant rite, climaxing in a covenant meal, and a vision of the God of Israel. The second unit (vv. 12–15a) concentrates on Yahweh's personal role in writing and handing over his law on two tablets of stone. The third section (vv. 15b–18) revolves around the unique mode of Yahweh's appearance on the mountain as a mysterious presence that looks like fire hidden behind a cloud. Thus each unit has a different perspective of God's relationship to his people at Sinai.

The preceding analysis may not be sufficient, however, to convince the literary critic that three literary hands are present in Exodus 24. He wants the supporting evidence of literary style and terminology. Are there any key terms, phrases, or grammatical constructions in one unit that set it apart as distinct in one way or another? The critic will observe, for example, that the writer of the first unit (vv. 1–11) speaks of the leaders seeing God. While that in itself may be significant, this writer uses the word Elohim for God at that point, despite the fact that Yahweh had already been revealed as the name for Israel's God (Exod. 6:2 ff.). By contrast, the writer of the third unit (vv. 15b–18) carefully avoids saying that Israel saw God. The people saw the glory (*kabod*) of Yahweh, not Yahweh himself. Even then, the *kabod Yahweh* was carefully veiled by its enveloping cloud. The term *Elohim* and the expression *kabod Yahweh* are but two illustrations of the kind of literary clues that the critic must uncover as he sifts the language of the text.

Assuming for the moment that there are three literary compositions evident in Exodus 24, do they stand alone? Or are they pieces of three larger literary works? Can three or more literary strata be traced throughout the Pentateuch?

3

The term *Elohim*, the covenant meal motif and the vision of God concept may suggest to the critic a connection between the first unit (Exod. 24:1-11) and the alleged Elohist source of the Pentateuch.[3] Threads of continuity between this first unit of Exodus 24 (vv. 1-11) and Exodus 18, which is regularly considered an Elohist text, can be readily detected. There, too, the elders are central and participate in a communal meal with Moses before God. God, moreover, is designated by the name Elohim. The obvious context for the second unit (Exod. 24:12-15a) is the narrative of Exodus 32. In that chapter Moses and Joshua descend Mount Sinai together, carrying the two tablets of stone. Aaron and those who remain behind, however, were unable to prevent the idolatrous revolt of God's people. Many literary critics connect this sequence with the Yahwist, a second major literary source that critics found throughout much of the Pentateuch.[4] Expressions like the *kabod Yahweh*, "settling" on Sinai, and the seventh day found in the third unit of Exodus 24 (vv. 15b-18) are considered typical elements of another source known as the Priestly Writing. In short, Exodus 24 seems to be composed of materials that belong to three larger literary complexes within the Pentateuch. In this way the literary critic searches for written stages of composition in a given passage or book. In the case of the Pentateuch he needs to test the widely accepted theory that four major written sources can be traced from Genesis through Deuteronomy.[5] Of these the Elohist is so named because the writer has a strong preference for Elohim as the name for God, even after the name Yahweh is revealed to Moses (Exodus 6). The Yahwist has the opposite tendency and regularly employs the name Yahweh for God in texts that precede the announcement of Yahweh's name to Moses in Exodus 6. The Priestly Writing is characterized by its interest in mat-

3. One of the most complete literary critical analyses of the Sinai traditions has been done by Walter Beyerlin, *Origins and History of the Oldest Sinaitic Traditions* (Oxford: Blackwell, 1961). He recognizes two stages of Elohist composition in Exodus 24:1-11.

4. While the contours of the Yahwist source are rather clearly defined in Genesis, there is some uncertainty among scholars as to the extent of the Yahwist in the Sinai context. In the opinion of this writer, Exodus 24:15b-18 and most of Exodus 32:1-20 belong to the Yahwist source.

5. The original concept of these sources derives largely from the work of a French professor of medicine called Astruc. As an old man he published anonymously his Latin work, *Conjectures on the Reminiscences which Moses Appears to have Used in Composing the Book of Genesis* (1753). He proposed a Jehovah (Yahweh) source and an Elohim source to account for most of the material in Genesis and several non-Israelite and supplementary sources for the remainder of the book.

4

ters of worship, while the Deuteronomist is found largely in the book of Deuteronomy. The Elohist is the most difficult of these sources to establish as a continuous literary work and deserves far more attention than we are able to give in this limited study.[6] These four sources are usually referred to by the symbols J (Yahwist), E (Elohist), D (Deuteronomist), and P (Priestly Writing).

Having neatly divided the text into literary sources, the literary critic today will be challenged by the form critic and the redaction critic.[7] The form critic will dispute the idea that the various units of the text necessarily arose at the hands of a literary composer. Form criticism poses a fresh set of questions. Did the text, or portion thereof, once exist in oral form? Is that form discernible as a common oral mode of communication in the ancient world? Is there a hymn or legend in the text that may have been transmitted by word of mouth for a certain period of time? What was the human situation that gave rise to the form in question? Was it a worship context, a wedding, or a court trial setting? The form critic who studies Exodus 24:1-11 will suggest, for example, that the text is more than a written report of a covenant ceremony at Sinai. He may propose that covenant ceremonies themselves have helped to shape the story as the Sinai experiences were related orally over the years. Expressions such as "all that Yahweh has spoken we will do" (Exod. 24:3, 7; 19:8), are seen as fixed responses from the formal worship life of later Israel that have been incorporated into the account. Hence the text is thought to have developed in a specific living situation such as the renewal of the covenant by the twelve tribes of Israel.

Even if we grant oral stages of growth for segments of the text, are the three units of Exodus 24 free from any evidence of literary activity? Are there signs that later interpreters modified the original units, whether oral or written? And how, in the last analysis, did these three units come to be arranged as they are? Is the Priestly Writing a final redaction of the Sinai materials? Did this literary work provide their chronological introduction in Exodus 19:1-2a? Did the Priestly Writing deliberately interpret "seeing God" in the

6. A good summary of the character and text of the Elohist is provided by Norman Gottwald, *A Light to the Nations* (New York: Harper, 1959), pp. 246-54.

7. For an illustration of the methodology of form criticism and redaction criticism in operation see K. Koch, *The Growth of Biblical Tradition* (New York: Charles Scribner's Sons, 1969).

first unit (Exod. 24:9–11) as viewing the glory of God (*kabod Yahweh*) partially hidden behind its cloud (Exod. 24:16–17)? Investigations of this nature are characteristic of redaction criticism. This discipline is one phase of tradition criticism which attempts to trace the history of each significant expression, formula, concept, oral form, literary unit, or literary source through the various stages of its development. Form criticism and redaction criticism are treated separately in this series.

Our presentation of literary criticism must take into account the implications of both these disciplines. We can no longer divide up the text into several literary sources and assume that we have discovered all the secrets of its origin. Yet the discipline of literary criticism still remains basic for any critical analysis of a given book or portion of the Old Testament.[8] In the light of our preceding portrait of the literary critic at work on Exodus 24, Old Testament literary criticism in the traditional sense can be defined as the task of analyzing the literary features of a given document to determine its literary character, origins, and states of written composition. The literary critic is concerned about whether a text is the work of one man or several, whether literary sources have been used, and whether editors have reworked the text in some way. The methodological clues suggested by our brief introduction to some of the literary development of Exodus 24 are applicable to larger literary complexes and complete documents.

The methodology of the literary critic can be outlined as follows. He begins by ascertaining the internal arrangement of the text chosen for study. What are its themes, structure, and literary units? How are these units related? Is there a thematic, formal, chronological, or haphazard connection between them? In posing these questions the critic may discover that more than one sequence of motifs or incidents is developed in the same document. He may then proceed to trace these elements through a series of passages in the document concerned. In so doing he may be led to ask additional questions. Are there logical or thematic inconsistencies within the document? Is one unit interrupted by a digression or secondary comment? Is there a sudden change in literary style? Do variant versions of the same account appear in the

8. Great Old Testament scholars such as Martin Noth, Gerhard von Rad and Sigmund Mowinckel were all, first of all, literary and historical critics. For them a basic literary source hypothesis remained fundamental for any study of the Pentateuch. See the Bibliography.

document? Do specific groupings of words keep reappearing in different contexts? Is a definite viewpoint espoused, lost, and then reaffirmed later in the same text? Examples of this methodology are isolated in the second portion of this chapter.

After the literary critic has assembled and assessed all the evidence gleaned from this procedure, he may be in a position to propose a hypothesis concerning the origins and composition of the document under scrutiny. This hypothesis must be tested on the document as a whole and on each of its parts. The value of the hypothesis will depend upon the validity of the evidence cited and the contribution the theory makes to a richer appreciation of the document under examination. Literary criticism is to provide the literary spadework for a better understanding of the function and import of a document. The critic, however, must guard against arguing too quickly from modern literary techniques in the assessment of an ancient text like the Old Testament. In ancient times sources of an oral or written nature were normally used without reference to their origin. Many works seem to have been composed by several authors over a long period of time. Editors apparently modified the work of their forefathers so as to bring them up to date or promote a new point of view. Thus the literary critic should also try to relate his literary findings to their historical context. To do this he will need to use all the pertinent information at his disposal about the language, culture, history, thought forms, and religions of the ancient world.

Some students may feel uncomfortable with terms such as *hypothesis* or *critical* in the study of the Old Testament. However, even the traditional claim that Moses wrote the Pentateuch is a hypothesis based on a critical evaluation of certain biblical passages. The theory that several literary sources can be found in the Pentateuch does not deny the role of Moses as the great human authority behind its content or the great antiquity of much of its text. We should also recognize that the Old Testament itself testifies to the use of specific written sources by some of its authors. The author of Numbers, for example, quotes from an unknown text which he designates *The Book of the Wars of Yahweh* (Num. 21:14).[9] Our commitment to the message of the Old Testament urges us to use every tool available to discern the full meaning of the biblical text. In that process it seems to us that literary criticism remains a vital discipline.

9. For additional examples see Joshua 10:12-13; 2 Samuel 1:18; 1 Kings 11:41; 14:19; 15:31; 16:14; and Ezra 1:2-4.

EXAMPLES OF LITERARY CRITICISM

The following examples are designed to supplement the preceding introduction to literary criticism. They offer concrete illustrations of the kind of evidence and techniques employed in a literary critical study of the Old Testament. Each of the various techniques is isolated here for the sake of clarity. As we investigate the possible literary sources of the Pentateuch in the next chapter, all of these techniques will be applied in a common literary context.

Comparing parallel accounts

Any student who reads through the Pentateuch will notice a striking similarity in certain stories. The same incident or speech seems to be reported in several ways. Repetition as such is a relatively common literary device in the literature of the ancient Near East as the old myths and legends of Canaan admirably testify. It is also true that some stories and sayings were retold orally by different tribes and peoples for centuries. Differing versions of the same story may therefore be due to the emphases which they acquired in their preliterary stage. Both of these factors contribute to the divergent forms of narrative and law within the Pentateuch. Yet these explanations hardly account for all of the evidence at hand either in the Pentateuch or elsewhere in the Scriptures. Literary factors also play a part.

The Old Testament literary critic has the good fortune of possessing two variant accounts of the history of Judah. The one is preserved in the books of Samuel and Kings and the other in 1 and 2 Chronicles. Each work begins with a common stock of tradition. For the Chronicler (as the author of Chronicles is usually called) this stock included a literary document that seems to have been the existing book of Samuel-Kings, or something very close to it. In his account of the history of Judah the Chronicler begins by eliminating all materials pertaining to Israel which have no direct bearing on the history of Judah and the temple. He treats his materials from a cultic rather than a political or historical point of view. The famous dynastic promise delivered by Nathan to David offers a clear illustration of how the writers of Samuel-Kings and Chronicles modify a common source to accent their own concerns. Consider the following comparison of Nathan's oracle as it appears in 2 Samuel 7 and 1 Chronicles 17:

8

2 Samuel 7	1 Chronicles 17
[11] *I will give you rest* from all your enemies.	[10] *I will subdue* all your enemies.
Moreover the Lord declares to you that the Lord will *make you a house.*	Moreover I declare to you that the Lord will *build you a house.*
[12] When your days are fulfilled and you *lie down* with your fathers, I will raise up your offspring after you, *who shall come forth from your body,* and I will establish his kingdom.	[11] When your days are fulfilled to *go to be* with your fathers, I will raise up your offspring after you, *one of your sons,* and I will establish his kingdom.
[13] He shall build a house *for my name,* and I will establish the throne *of his kingdom* forever.	[12] He shall build a house *for me,* and I will establish his throne forever.
[14] I will be his father and he shall be my son. *When he commits iniquity, I will chasten him with the rod of men, with the stripes of the sons of men.*	[13] I will be his father and he will by my son. (No parallel to 2 Sam. 7:14b)
[15] But I will not take my steadfast love from him, as I took it from *Saul, whom I put away from before you.*	I will not take my steadfast love from him, as I took it from him who was before you.
[16] And *your house* and *your kingdom* shall be *made sure* forever before me; your throne shall be established forever.	[14] But I will *confirm* him in *my house* and in *my kingdom* forever and his throne shall be established forever.

Some of the variations in these two versions of Nathan's oracle to David may be purely stylistic. But many of the differences reflect the distinct viewpoint of the writer. It is evident elsewhere that the Chronicler portrays David in a good light. The evils and errors of both David and Solomon are carefully omitted. It is natural therefore that the unfavorable reference to chastisement for iniquity in 2 Samuel 7:14b would be omitted from the Chronicler's rendering. This is true despite that fact that the other ancient version of this oracle in Psalm 89 includes this allusion to the sins of David's house (Ps. 89:32).

For the Chronicler the temple and its cult are central. This concern helps to explain why 1 Chronicles 17:14 reads "in my house." This house is obviously the temple, while the "house" in the parallel text of 2 Samuel 7:16 is the dynasty of David, not the temple. Further, the deliberate choice of the verb "build" in 1 Chronicles 17:10 likewise hints at the construction of the temple, since that verb can mean either the building of a house or the establishing of a dynasty. The

9

writer of Samuel-Kings employs the less ambiguous "make" at this point thereby focusing on the dynasty rather than the temple. Or again, peace and rest are tied to the promise of the Davidic dynasty in 2 Samuel 7:11, but for the Chronicler such peace and rest coincide with the building of the temple and the work of Solomon (1 Chron. 22:6–10), not with the dynastic promise to David. Therefore, 1 Chronicles 17:10 speaks of David's role in terms of warfare. He is to "subdue" his enemies rather than enjoy "rest."

These few illustrations from one parallel between Samuel-Kings and Chronicles demonstrate the importance of variations between one account and another. Numerous similar parallels between Samuel-Kings and Chronicles could be cited. In the Pentateuch, however, parallel accounts of the same tradition may appear within the same book. In some cases two versions of the same story seem to have been combined into one account. In other words, it is not sufficient to grant the possibility of duplicate accounts based on the analogy of Samuel-Kings and Chronicles. We must also discern where the varying accounts begin and end. If we assume that we have a writer like the compiler of Samuel-Kings and another writer like the Chronicler whose two works were combined into one book, or series of books, how can we distinguish the work of each of these authors? That is a second critical phase which we must pursue later in our literary analysis of the Pentateuch.

Distinguishing Combined Accounts

In some cases the parallel accounts in the Pentateuch are as obvious as they are in a comparison of Chronicles with Samuel-Kings. In such cases divergent style, viewpoint, or terminology can be easily investigated. Where two versions of the same story are combined into one account this division of literary sources is more difficult. Let us use 1 Samuel 17 as an example. If we read 1 Samuel 17 omitting verses 12–31, 41, 50 and 55–58 we have a complete story which is consistent with the preceding David narratives. In chapter 16 David and his household are introduced. David is anointed and enters the service of Saul's court where he plays the lyre with great skill. Finally David joins Saul's army and becomes his armor bearer (1 Sam. 16:21). In that capacity David obtains permission from Saul to fight the Philistine (1 Sam. 17:37). After his great victory he returns to Jerusalem with the head of Goliath (1 Sam. 17:54).

If, however, we read 1 Samuel 17:12–31, 41, 50 and 55–

58 separately, we gain a rather different portrait of the situation. There are several signs that these verses belong to a different version of the David and Goliath episode. In this version David and his household are introduced a second time (1 Sam. 17:12 ff.). Here David is an unknown shepherd boy tending his sheep. He is called upon to send provisions to his brothers on the battlefield (1 Sam. 17:20). The setting for the battle is provided a second time and the giant again identified by name as Goliath (1 Sam. 17:19, 23). David's father is introduced as an Ephrathite of Bethlehem with eight sons (1 Sam. 17:12-15). This introduction conflicts with the introduction of 1 Samuel 16 where Jesse and his family are well known to the reader. In chapter 16 David is already in the service of Saul and engaged as his personal armor bearer. In that context the personal bond between Saul and David is made even closer by David's lyre playing. This alternate introduction of 1 Samuel 17:12 ff., is balanced by a second conclusion in 1 Samuel 17:55-18:5. According to this conclusion David is still unknown to Saul, but after the victory he prospers in Saul's service until he becomes commander of the Israelite warriors. The second introduction and conclusion grow out of a totally different frame of reference than the first. In the one account Israel is saved by Saul's personal companion and inevitable successor. In the other David's deed is a spontaneous act by an unknown savior similar to the saviors like Gideon and Jephthah who preceded David in Israel.

Passages like these which break the sequence of a narrative and reflect a conflicting situation may offer evidence of two versions of the same story. Sometimes these versions may have been conflated or combined before they were written down and edited by an author. In the case of 1 Samuel 17, however, the intrusive verses cited seem to belong to an alternate literary tradition since they are absent from one major ancient text of the Septuagint, the early Greek translation of the Old Testament. It is this kind of break in the narrative, this kind of divergent introduction or conclusion, and this kind of contradictory situation or perspective that offer clues for combined literary sources.

Recognizing Literary Terminology

Another earmark of a literary source or school of writers is a definite style and set of terminology which characterizes the writer or writers involved. When the same words or expressions are repeatedly found in the same order and man-

11

ner a distinct literary hand or tradition is suggested. By observing these features, a student today can readily identify the lecture notes of one professor from those of another. Most writers tend to develop a style and a jargon of their own. The style and jargon of Deuteronomy are very obvious. They stand in sharp contrast to the literary characteristics of the rest of the Pentateuch. When compared with Genesis through Numbers, Deuteronomy presents a new world of terms, thought patterns, groups of expressions, and stereotype idioms. If the reader works through Deuteronomy 4-11, for example, he is met by the style of a preacher. This preacher urges his audience over and over again to keep the laws set before them. He makes urgent appeals to the will of his listeners by using familiar phrases. If we focus our attention on Deuteronomy 11, which represents a kind of concluding sermon preceding the law code of Deuteronomy 12-26, we can observe this writer clearly and hear this preacher coming through forcefully. The abbreviated translation of Deuteronomy 11 which follows italicizes those idioms or groups of terms which occur frequently throughout Deuteronomy but are absent or rare elsewhere in the Pentateuch. These expressions are translated here in such a way as to reflect the special style of writing in the Hebrew original.

¹*And you shall love Yahweh your God,*
and you shall keep his charge (literally: what is to be kept)
and his statutes and his judgments and his commandments
all the days
²And consider *this day*
(since I am not speaking to your children who have not
known or seen it) the discipline of *Yahweh your God*, his
greatness, his mighty hand and his outstretched arm . . . .
⁷*For your eyes have seen*
all the great *work* of Yahweh *which he worked.*
⁸*And you shall keep*
the commandment which I am commanding you this day
that you may be strong and enter
and inherit the land you are passing over to inherit it,
⁹*that your days may be long on the land,*
which Yahweh swore to your fathers to give to them and to
their seed, a land flowing with milk and honey.
¹⁰For *the land which you are entering to inherit it*
is not like the land of Egypt . . .

12

[13]And if you really obey
my commandment which I am commanding you this day,
to love Yahweh your God
and to serve him *with all your heart and all your soul,*
[14]he will give the rain for your land in its season
the early rain and the latter rain,
that you may gather in your wine, your grain and your oil,
[15]And he will give grass in your fields for your cattle,
and you shall eat and be full.
[16]*Take heed to yourself lest* your heart be deceived
and you turn aside *and you serve other gods and you*
worship them,
[17]and the anger of Yahweh be kindled against you
and he shut up the heavens so that there be no rain,
and the land yield no fruit
and you perish quickly off *the good land*
which Yahweh gives you . . .
[22]For if you *really keep*
all this commandment which I am commanding you to do,
to love Yahweh your God
to walk in all his ways and *cleave to him,*
[23]then Yahweh will drive out all these nations . . .
[26]Behold I set before you this day a blessing and a curse;
[27]the blessing: *if you obey the commandments of Yahweh*
your God which I am commanding you, this day,
[28]and the curse: *if you do not obey the commandments of*
Yahweh your God and turn aside from the way
which I am commanding you this day
to go after other gods
which you have not known.

A glance at the preceding text reveals not only recurring expressions such as "this day," but a certain way of writing. For example, we meet the same verbal root within a given group of words. Thus we read, "my *commandment* which I am *commanding*," "*inherit* the land you are passing over to *inherit*," "the *work* which Yahweh *worked*," or "*keep* what is to be *kept*." Redundant infinitives appear in expressions such as "passing over *to inherit*" and "commanding you *to do*." Another feature is the heaping up of parallel or related words. Thus the Israelite is to keep "his charge and his statutes and his judgments and his commandments." He is to consider Yahweh's "discipline, his greatness, his mighty arm and his outstretched hand." Doing this will enable him

13

to "be strong and enter and inherit" the land. In the last analysis the Israelite is to love Yahweh, "with all his heart, all his soul and all his might."

A similar mode of emphasizing his major interests is demonstrated in the way this writer describes the land. He is never satisfied to speak of the land as such, or to refer to the land of Canaan. The land is repeatedly portrayed as, "the good land," "the land flowing with milk and honey," "the land which Yahweh swore to your fathers to give," or "the land which you are passing over to inherit it." Similarly the people of God are not merely the people or the community, but "a holy people," "a people of special posses-. sion," or a "people of his own possession." There is no need to belabor the point. When this writer goes into one of his exhortations to obey the commandments of Yahweh he falls into his stock of stereotype idioms about obedience, blessings of obedience, kinds of sin, and the curses of disobedience. Wherever this collection of phrases with this sermonic style appears, we seem to have the evidence of a definite literary tradition. This fact strongly suggests that Deuteronomy stems from a different literary context than the other parts of the Pentateuch which do not exhibit this style and language.

Discerning Literary Structures

This kind of evidence can be supplemented by indications of a continuous grouping of expressions or a recurring literary structure. Such a literary pattern is evident in the book of Judges. In Judges 2:11–23 the author gives the rationale for his interpretation of the era of the judges. The pattern of history discerned by this author also suggests a literary structure for his portrayal of each of the judges. In this pattern the same set of expressions keeps repeating and offers clear evidence of his literary hand. The basic pattern is as follows:

> The sons of Israel *did what was evil in the sight of Yahweh* . . .
> *And they served* Baals (or some other gods) . . .
> *Therefore the anger of Yahweh was kindled* against Israel.
> *So he sold them into the hand of*———*for*———*years.*
> Then the sons of Israel *cried to Yahweh for help* . . .
> And *Yahweh raised up a deliverer* for the sons of Israel. . . .

14

This structure appears in its simplest form in Judges 3:7-11. With variations the same pattern is employed in Judges 3:12 ff., 4:1 ff., 6:1 ff., 10:6 ff., 13:1 ff. The literary expressions italicized in the outline above are usually repeated verbatim each time the pattern reappears. This literary structure is expanded to provide a theological rationale for the writer's interpretation of the entire history of the judges in the preface of Judges 2:11-23. A comparable literary structure is evident in the treatment of the kings of Israel and Judah throughout the book of Kings. In the case of the kings of Judah the following sequence is regularly used to introduce a king:

Year of office of the reigning king of Israel.
Name of the king of Judah and his father.
Age at date of accession and duration of reign.
Name of the mother of king of Judah.
Judgment on his religious activities.

Examples of this formal introductory sequence appear in 2 Kings 14:1-3; 15:1-3; 16:1-3; 18:1-3 and elsewhere. A similar formulation concludes the reign of each of the kings of Judah, indicating where the rest of his deeds are recorded, stating that the king slept with his fathers in the city of David, and reporting the name of his son who became king. Structure, patterns, or stereotype arrangements of this nature are the earmarks of a literary author. They reflect a literary organization of material into a meaningful order. The preliminary basis for such an order offered in Judges 2:11-23 supports the conclusion that the arrangement is a deliberate literary design rather than the repetition of some oral form. In the case of the writer of Kings, repeated reference is made to literary sources of information available to the author. A similar search for literary patterns, stereotype expressions and recurring sets of terminology will be part of our literary investigation of the Pentateuch.

Establishing Divergent Viewpoints

The presence of a second literary hand is sometimes evident in a distinctive way of thinking or theological stance. Where a definite change in theological approach is accompanied by other indications of a different literary hand the likelihood of a second literary source is greatly increased. An example from Jeremiah 33 may help to reinforce the point. Jeremiah 33:14-26 seems to reflect a position which

15

stands in tension with the message proclaimed by Jeremiah elsewhere in his book. Jeremiah was critical of the priesthood and temple of Jerusalem. He predicted the fall of the temple and the city of Jerusalem. Anything which made the temple, its personnel, or the city itself an external guarantee of God's presence was condemned by Jeremiah. Jeremiah demanded the personal faithfulness of God's people to the covenant relationship established by God himself (see Jer. 7:1–15; 4:1–4; 23:33–40).

With Jeremiah 33:14–26 the accent has changed. Jerusalem and the priesthood play a central role in the new age. Sacrifices are to be offered forever as part of the eternal priesthood of the Levitical priests who had never been mentioned by this name elsewhere in Jeremiah. This new focus on Zion as the central symbol of God's grace is seen in the rewording of the famous messianic promise from Jeremiah 23:5–6. The title "Yahweh is our Righteousness" was there applied to the future king. In Jeremiah 33:16 it is applied to Jerusalem who is promised security under the new future of God with his people. This antithesis between condemning Zion as a false symbol of security and making Zion a central symbol of hope can hardly be ignored. These emphases appear to be indicative of two different theological approaches to the role of Zion, temple, and priesthood for God's people. That this reflects two literary hands seems to be confirmed by the fact that the text of Jeremiah 33:14–26 is not part of the Septuagint text of Jeremiah.

Tracing Normative Motifs

Literary appreciation involves more than a neat division of sources into divergent literary strata. Nor can one be satisfied with asserting that two conflicting viewpoints coexist in a given segment of material. One must search for a progression of thought and theme, a significant development of normative motifs, or a definite programmatic use of certain governing ideas. Dimensions of this nature often give a work its unifying character. If we have literary artists or sources in the Pentateuch we must analyze their literary design and thematic control. We must allow language, terminology, viewpoint, and all other literary characteristics to remain an integrated part of a total work whose import is conveyed by the centralizing elements and not become obsessed with a handful of favorite identification marks.

One cannot read through the book of Ecclesiastes without realizing that the opening affirmation and question present a governing or programmatic concept to be tested and developed in the rest of the book. "Vanity of vanities," says the Preacher, "vanity of vanities. All is vanity. What does a man gain by all the toil at which he toils under the sun?" This opening cry (Eccles. 1:2-3) governs the whole attitude and thought progression of the writer. After a long resume of all his efforts to find meaning in life this great skeptic announces his discovery: "Then I considered all that my hands had done and the toil I had spent in doing it, and behold all was vanity and a striving after wind, and there was nothing new to be gained under the sun" (Eccles. 2:11). A wide range of themes is treated in relation to this one central concern over the futility and vanity of life. One can recognize here far more than a pessimistic viewpoint or a propensity for the term *vanity*. Living, dying, wisdom, and similar weighty subjects are developed in the light of this one overriding theme. One climactic assertion which draws the writer's feelings to a pointed conclusion about this theme appears in Ecclesiastes 9:9-10:

Enjoy life with your wife whom you love all the days of your vain life which he has given you under the sun, because that is your portion in life and in your toil which you toil under the sun. Whatever your hands find to do, do it with your might; for there is no work or thought or knowledge or wisdom in Sheol to which you are going.

Chapters three and four of this book will emphasize this technique of tracing normative motifs as a means of gaining a richer sensitivity to the full dimensions of the literary source under scrutiny.

The preceding examples of literary critical evidence offer preliminary indications of what the literary critic will seek as he works through the Pentateuch. In the next chapter we shall apply these literary critical techniques to the text of Genesis 1-11. In the following chapters we shall focus upon the character of the Pentateuchal sources we have identified by studying their treatment of central themes. We have chosen to demonstrate the literary critical process in the Pentateuch precisely because it is at that point in the biblical record where the greatest controversies have raged over the use of this discipline and where the coolest reason must still prevail.

II
Discovering Literary Sources

Genesis is still a good place to begin reading the Old Testament. And Genesis 1–9 is a suitable location in the Pentateuch to illustrate the process of literary criticism. What literary sources and characteristics can be isolated in these chapters by using the techniques of literary analysis introduced above? What contributions to the understanding of this crucial portion of the Scriptures are made by such an analysis? These are the basic questions to which we shall address ourselves in this chapter. The general categories for investigating the literary evidence involved will be those of style, terminology, and perspective. Under the first category we shall consider writing technique, structural arrangement, and use of language. Under the second we shall give attention to recurring terms, names, key expressions, and clusters of words. Under the third we shall focus upon the central thrust, outlook, or vantage point of a specific section.

A search for oral forms or preliterary traditions may operate with much of the same evidence and some of the same methods demonstrated here. The recognition of a literary source or literary tradition, however, demands that we uncover a continuity of related literary evidence in an extended sequence of passages. The plausibility of a literary hand depends on the evidence of a common style, a related set of terminology, a generally consistent perspective, and/or a literary superstructure over a series of literary contexts. Such is the broader task of literary criticism. By a simple inductive study of Genesis 1–9 we plan to illustrate this process and isolate the evidence for two major literary sources.

ISOLATING THE EVIDENCE OF GENESIS 1–5
Literary Style

Differences in literary style are sometimes easier to feel than to define. The listener in the pew can often recognize the difference in the style of one preacher from that of another without being able to verbalize the precise nature of the difference. One preacher may employ a conversational approach while another may operate as a dramatic herald.

Each contemporary author too has his own style and a description of that style should be possible even if not comprehensive. Similar variations in style are to be found in ancient authors. A careful survey of the Pentateuch discloses a diversity of stylistic features.

Differences in style between Genesis 1 and most of Genesis 2 are immediately apparent. Genesis 1 is repetitious, tabular, and formal. Not only do certain words and expressions keep repeating but each of the days of creation are reported in much the same way. The events of each day are set into a fixed pattern which does not change. This pattern or framework has been summarized by Westermann[1] as follows:

Announcement: And God said . . .
Command: Let there be . . . and let . . .
Report: And it was so!
Evaluation: And God saw that it was good.
Temporal Framework: And there was evening and there
                       was morning, the . . . day.

The writer of the creation account has organized each of the six days into a structure that expresses order and planning for each day. In the broader structure we see a tenfold announcement of God. Ten times we hear, "And God said . . ." followed by the resultant creative movement from chaos to order. This arrangement of the materials is like a catalog of all the major units of the cosmos.

But the style is more than that of a cataloger. There is a kind of authority in the brevity and form of the repeated elements like, "Let there be . . .," "It was so," or "And God saw that it was good." And there is a certain solemn majesty about the tone of the entire account. This structure and tone stands in contrast to most of the creation accounts of the ancient Near East. In these myths there is a story with characters, plot, and conflict. Such myths reflect the annual drama between the gods of chaos and the gods of creation. In Genesis 1 the mood has changed. Instead of a drama there is a series of solemn announcements or commands. Some of these announcements may, however, reflect a polemic against the creation myths of the ancient Near East. Expressions like, "face of the deep," "the greater light,"

1. C. Westermann, *The Genesis Accounts of Creation* (Philadelphia: Fortress Press, 1964), pp. 1–7. For a fine popular treatment of the early chapters of Genesis according to their literary sources see T. E. Fretheim, *Creation, Fall and Flood* (Minneapolis: Augsburg, 1969).

or "the great sea monsters" suggest an underlying polemic consistent with the style and structure of this account of creation.[2] The style of the creation text of Genesis 1:1–2:4a, therefore, seems to be that of someone ordering his materials into a series of similar solemn commands in such a way that the authority of the one giving the command stands unchallenged, and the content of his commands presents a comprehensive catalog of the major divisions of the created world known to the writer.

A second creation text seems to begin in Genesis 2:4b with a temporal introduction, "In the day that. . . ." A temporal introduction had appeared in Genesis 1:1 as "When God began to create . . ." or "In the beginning God created. . . ." Similar expressions introduce other creation accounts of the ancient world. After the new beginning of Genesis 2:4b we meet a sudden switch in form and style. The creation text of Genesis 2:4b–25 is a story with a sequel in Genesis 3:1–24. The relationship of the characters rather than the tabulation of events or commands is primary here. The language is picturesque and flowing. The various acts of God the creator are closely interrelated rather than separated by distinct periods of time or repeated expressions such as "It was so," or "It was good." In Genesis 2:4b–25 there is no uniform framework for each act of God. The creative workings of God are interdependent parts of one story.

Evocative poetic terms such as "mist," "rib," "deep sleep," and "cleave" abound in this account. These terms appeal to the imagination and enable the reader to visualize the creation scene more readily. At this point a knowledge of the Hebrew text proves advantageous. The colorful scene portrayed in Genesis 2:5–7 is that of God laboring like a potter or sculptor in the midst of a desert land free from vegetation. There he "molds" man as a potter would mold a piece of clay. From this clay he forms a model, draws it to himself and breathes life into its nostrils. In so doing he seems to reflect the ancient practice of mouth-to-mouth breathing (cf. 2 Kings 4:34). No two creative acts are alike in Genesis 2:4b–25. None of the creative activities of God are preceded by the formal divine command found in Genesis 1. On the one occasion when God does speak before

2. See below under Theological Perspective. Polemical elements in the creation narrative in no way eliminate the possibility that the order of the creation events was originally borrowed from ancient Near Eastern myth traditions such as those of the Enuma Elish of Babylon.

creating woman, he is portrayed as speaking to himself about the situation. "It is not good for man to be alone," he muses. Such a statement is in contrast to the affirmations of Genesis 1: "And God said: 'Let there be . . .!'" The same kind of flowing narrative and style continues through Genesis 4:16, where a similar economy of words is evident. The dramatic dimension of this story is increased by the introduction of dialogue. "Did God say?" asks the snake. "We can eat!" retorts the woman. "But you won't really die," adds the snake. These conversations make this account far more than a dry report and completely unlike the catalog of commands in Genesis 1. Thus in Genesis 2:4b–4:16 we meet concise and vivid stories told in a masterful fashion.

When the reader reaches Genesis 5, however, he is confronted with a genealogy which exhibits a structured tabular form. The life of each individual in the genealogy is summarized with the same outline and fixed set of expressions. This process reminds us of the tabular format employed in the creation sequence of Genesis 1. The pattern for each primeval hero in Genesis 5 can be seen in the following summary:

> When A had lived . . . years he became the
> father of B . . .
> A lived . . . years after the birth of B . . .
> and he had sons and daughters . . .
> thus all the days of A were . . .
> and he died!

A second look at Genesis 5 reveals the presence of a formal introduction: "This is the book of the generations (toledot) of Adam." A comparable statement seems to provide a conclusion to the creation story in Genesis 2:4a. A survey of Genesis discloses a number of similar introductory statements pertaining to the generations of the heroes of Genesis (6:9; 10:1; 11:27; etc.). This evidence suggests the possibility that the same formal method of structuring the story of the creation in Genesis 1 and the ordering of the family history of the ancestors in Genesis 5 may be part of a literary superstructure for all of Genesis.

One frequent reaction of students to any claim of divergent style is an appeal to divergent subject matter. This argument needs to be tested by specific cases. One may readily assume that a genealogy, by virtue of its very nature, will be structured or rigid in its form and dull or monotonous in style. However, a glance at the genealogy of Genesis 4:17-25 demonstrates that the opposite is possible. In addition to variant ways of describing the several family relationships involved, this text is interspersed with items of human interest. These prevent the genealogy from becoming a dry tabulation of names and figures. Enoch is said to have built a city, Lamech is credited with two wives, Jabal is the first tent dweller, and Tubal-cain is introduced as the first man to forge metal instruments. Nor is it possible to demand that the subject matter of Genesis 1 necessarily dictated the style of writing employed. Essentially the same acts and sequence of creation appear in Psalm 104 where the poetic style and form of writing are totally different.

In recent times the discipline of form criticism has raised the question of whether we can speak of literary style at all. Are not the differences between the creation texts of Genesis 1 and 2, for example, explainable on the basis of the two literary forms which these chapters represent? To some extent this is true. However, we must raise the question of whether or not the isolation of literary forms is sufficient for an understanding of all the evidence involved. Genesis 4:17-26 and Genesis 5 have the same basic literary form, but reflect different methods of treating the material. Where a common literary form of the same story or material is presented with major differences in style and approach, the possibility exists that two different authors or traditions are at work. If we posit the presence of several authors in Genesis, we must also grant the possibility that one author may have a propensity for using one literary form rather than another, but to support such a hypothesis we must be able to see the evidence of his hand apart from the use of a particular literary form as such. To test this possibility we shall search through Genesis 1-5 again for the kind of recurring terminology which distinguishes the emphases and perspective of one group of materials from those of the other.

Distinctive Terminology

The difference in literary style between Genesis 1 and 5 on the one hand and Genesis 2:4b-4:26 on the other is complemented by the specific terminology used in these two sets of material. For the creative process Genesis 1 uses the term "create" (*bara'*) several times (1:1, 21, 27; 2:4a). Genesis 2 drops the term "create" in favor of the verb "form" (*yaṣar*) as in 2:7, 8, 19. The verb create first reappears in Genesis 5:1 and 2, a section which was previously linked with Genesis 1 on stylistic grounds. A second example of how these two sections differ is in the use of crucial terms defining the character of man. In Genesis 1 and 5 man is described as being in the "likeness" and the "image" of God (1:26–27 and 5:1–3). In Genesis 2, however, where the creation of man is the central subject, these two terms are absent and man is designated a "living being" (*nepesh ḥayah*), an expression also used to characterize the animals (2:7, 19). Genesis 1 and 5 speak of man as "male and female" (or "masculine and feminine") while Genesis 2 and 3 use the terms "man and woman."

These and similar terms or idioms for parallel ideas or subjects suggest the possibility of two minds at work. The possibility also exists that these variations in terminology are due to an oral situation where these materials were first formulated rather than to the literary hands which preserved or remolded them. The persistent appearance of the distinguishing terms and idioms in each of these groups of materials throughout other parts of Genesis must first be demonstrated if we are to substantiate the hypothesis of separate literary authors.

Perhaps the most important difference in terminology which persists throughout Genesis is found in the use of the divine names. Throughout Genesis 1:1–2:4a the name God (*Elohim*) is used to designate the deity. As soon as the style and subject changes in Genesis 2:4b, the expressions Lord (*Yahweh*) or Lord God (*Yahweh Elohim*) appear and continue through Genesis 4. With Genesis 5 *Elohim* again appears and *Yahweh* is again avoided. This usage demands some kind of explanation. Granting the theological significance of each of these names, the fact remains that the way in which these names are used is a major piece of literary evidence in the analysis of the book of Genesis. Yahweh is studiously avoided as a designation for God in those sections of Genesis which correspond to the style, terminology, and perspective of Genesis 1.[3] And this factor becomes another

3. The evidence needs to be stated clearly at this point. The materials consistent with Genesis 1 avoid the use of the term Yahweh until that name is revealed to Moses (Exod. 6:2 ff.). The materials consistent with Genesis 2:4b–26 do not necessarily avoid the term Elohim. On the contrary, where this writer himself mentions God, however, he normally uses Yahweh. The one verse in Genesis 1–5 which perhaps challenges our observations is Genesis 5:29. This verse seems to be a Yahwist intrusion into the Priestly genealogy of Genesis 5.

constant in the accumulation of evidence in favor of a consistent literary author in these portions of Genesis.

Theological Perspective

The preceding variations in style and terminology between the two groupings under discussion are balanced by a corresponding difference in theological interest or perspective. Were the texts under discussion not theological in content, this difference might be sought in the writer's attitude to life, nature, mankind, and similar concerns. To some extent also, divergencies of interest may be the natural outgrowth of variation in subject matter. But where the basic theological approach of two sections differs, we are led to search for something more than the topic involved for an explanation of the evidence.

The characterization of God differs markedly in the two sections of Genesis 1–5 under consideration. In Genesis 1 the majestic transcendence of a powerful cosmic organizer is primary. In line with this basic viewpoint Elohim creates and orders the universe by a series of decrees. He issues his command and the results are automatic. God appears as a being who stands outside of his cosmos and controls it with his mighty word. Hence the possible "anthropomorphic" expressions of Genesis 1 ("God said," "God saw," and "God rested") are reserved in character and tend to preserve the transcendence of God. They do not suggest the close proximity of a God who acts and looks like men.

Mankind in turn is created to rule the earth and act as God's vice-regent. He controls the earth for the sovereign overlord. "Then God said, 'Let us make man in our *image* after our likeness; and let them have *dominion* . . . over all the earth'" (Gen. 1:26). The image of God is that special character and relationship of man to God which enables him to represent God as the ruler of the earth. The divine blessing given to man empowers him to execute his function as God's representative by propagating his kind to fill and subdue the earth for which he is responsible. In Genesis 5 the same concept of the image and blessing of God is perpetuated in man's descendants (cf. Gen. 9:1–6). There is no indication that the events related in Genesis 2–4 affected this role of man as a being who is to exercise this special function. In other words, Genesis 5 seems to be a direct continuation of Genesis 1:1–2:4a both in terms of style and theological perspective. The image of God, in this sense, continues as a unifying concept in Genesis 5 and in Genesis 9:1–6.

In Genesis 2:4b–4:26 the portrait of God is very different. Here his immanence, personal nearness, and local involvement on the human scene are basic features. Yahweh is not a detached sovereign overlord but a God at hand as an intimate master. He is a God with whom man has ready contact and immediate responsibility. Accordingly the anthropomorphisms of Genesis 2–4 are so bold that they almost seem to depict Yahweh in terms of human limitations. He molds with his hands as a potter, he breathes into the mouth of a clay model, he plants a garden, he digs a rib from a man, he walks through a garden, he searches for a man, he has private conversations with man, woman, and beast, and he places a mark on yet another man. One almost gets the impression that he is experimenting and feeling his way as a creator. He discovers that "it is not good for man to be alone" and so he makes animals for man. But they are not the right company for man. "There was not found a helper fit for man." And so Yahweh makes a woman who proves to be an equal companion for man (Gen. 2:18–24).

The absence of the terms "image of God," "likeness," and "have dominion," in Genesis 2–4 is significant especially where the creation and character of man are central themes of the writer. The emphasis here does not lie on man as the authorized representative of God who rules the world on his behalf (as in Genesis 1) but, among other things, on man's close link with the ground. Man is distinguished from the animals in that he is personally addressed by Yahweh but he is one with the animals in terms of his origin from the dust of the ground. The repeated wordplay between "man" ('adam) and "ground" ('adamah) in Genesis 2:6, 7, 19; 3:17, 19; 4:11 emphasize this relationship. Terms like "dust," "form," and "living creature" (nepesh hayah) belong to the same complex of thought. The alienation of man from the ground is expressed by the term "curse" (in Gen. 3:14, 17; 4:11).

Many of these elements may reflect an agricultural perspective on the part of the writer. Man is viewed as a farmer and is condemned to labor as a man of the soil until he returns to the soil (Gen. 2:5; 3:17–19). The fig trees, the reference to Eden as a location "in the East," and the barrenness of the land after the fall suggest a Palestinian background for the writer of Genesis 2–4. Moreover the temptations and issues of life which the writer appears to be tracing through his narrative were especially pertinent to the Palestinian Israelites, and the polemic implied in his interpretation of the fall of man seems to be directed against the fertility cults of Canaan.[4]

The polemical accents of Genesis 1, however, are much different in intent. At several points in the creation sequence there appear polemics against mythical concepts of life which were integral to the creation theology of the ancient world. More specifically, the creation tradition reflected in ancient Near Eastern creation myths such as the *Enuma Elish* seems to be repudiated at certain points in Genesis 1. Thus, for example, it is hardly accidental that the sun (*shemesh*) and the moon (*yareaḥ*) which were names of Near Eastern deities, are not mentioned by name, but are referred to indirectly as the greater and lesser lights. The chaos monster (*tannin*) is not presented in Genesis 1:6-8 as the formidable foe which God had to conquer in order to divide the chaos waters, but rather sea monsters (*tannin*) appear on the fifth day as a kind of afterthought when the fish have been created. Likewise the chaos deep (Gen. 1:2) is no longer the archenemy of the creator God. Polemical elements appear throughout Genesis 1-4, but the background and orientation of the issue in Genesis 1 seem to be considerably different from those in Genesis 2-4.

A complete study of the theological, cultural and polemical dimensions of these chapters demands much more space than we have at our disposal. Suffice it to say that the differing viewpoints cited above do exist and contribute greatly to the significance and value of these materials. Whether this difference reflects the activity of two minds, two communities, or one mind on different occasions, or some other possibility, is for the reader to decide after weighing this and the subsequent evidence.

Summary

Most scholars have identified the proposed author of the materials in Genesis 1:1-2:4a and Genesis 5 as the Priestly Writer, primarily because of his later concern for the priesthood, the cult and worship activities. His treatment of the seventh day in Genesis 2:1-3 illustrates this concern. The second proposed author has been designated the Yahwist

4. See T. E. Fretheim, *Creation, Fall and Flood*, pp. 80–82. On snake worship in Israel see K. R. Jones, "The Bronze Serpent in the Israelite Cult," *JBL* 87 (1968): 245–56.

because he, in contrast to the Priestly Writer, regularly uses the name Yahweh for God prior to the time when that name was revealed to Moses in a special way (in Exod. 6:2 ff.). A tabular summary of the evidence from Genesis 1–5 discussed above is given below to provide a useful reference guide for the analysis of similar evidence in the subsequent chapters of Genesis.

DISTINGUISHING CATEGORY	GENESIS 1:1–2:4A AND GENESIS 5	GENESIS 2:4B–4:26
Style	solemn and majestic repetitive stereotype idioms balanced structures	story form—artistic economy of words picturesque and evocative dramatic use of dialogue
	appeals to the intellect	appeals to the imagination
Terminology	create (bara') image—likeness male and female the deep the waters sea monster (tannin) swarm ha'adam as mankind	form (yaṣar) living being man and woman the dust the ground ('adamah) snake (nahash) curse ha'adam as the first man
Idioms	(These are) the generations of . . . and God blessed and said . . . be fruitful and multiply . . . and fill the earth . . .	Cursed is . . . from the (face of) the ground . . .
	according to its kind . . . for food . . . God said . . . and it was so!	
The Divine Name	Elohim	Yahweh Yahweh Elohim
Theology	cosmic perspective	man the central concern
	the ordered world God as transcendent God majestic	the cursed ground God as immanent God intimate and involved
	restrained anthropomorphisms creation by word God as sovereign	bold anthropomorphisms creation by hand God as gracious

27

COMPARING THE EVIDENCE OF GENESIS 6-9

The evidence of Genesis 1-5 suggests the possibility of two different groups of materials. Additional evidence is demanded, however, if we are to make a balanced judgment as to whether two different traditions or authors are actually involved in these materials of Genesis. Accordingly we shall scrutinize the text of Genesis 6-9 in the light of the criteria and findings suggested by the study of Genesis 1-5 above. Several options exist as we approach the flood narrative of Genesis 6-9: (a) the story of the flood as a whole possesses a totally different style and character from either of the groupings in Genesis 1-5, (b) the entire flood narrative is consistent with one of these two groupings, (c) the flood narrative reflects two kinds of material which are consistent in character with the two groups in Genesis 1-5, (d) the flood account gives evidence of a multiplicity of sources, authors, and traditions, (e) the flood record is the unified work of one man. Our task is to determine which of these options seems the most plausible.

The Preface of Genesis 6:1-4

Genesis 6:1-4 includes a story which explains the presence of giants in the ancient world, and gives a reason for the short span of human life. This text is an independent unit which makes no specific allusion to the subsequent flood narrative or to the events which have preceded. The story, however, is not inappropriate at this juncture since it accentuates the corruption which existed on the earth and the preliminary steps which God had taken to curtail a perverted human domination (cf. Gen. 3:22-24). A connection with the gracious punishment motif of Genesis 3:22-24 is possible. Because of the brevity of the story any clear literary relationships are difficult to establish. The reference to the "face of the ground" in Genesis 6:1 suggests that there is a possible link with the materials of Genesis 2-4, and that this brief episode may have been incorporated into the sequence of primeval history by the author of Genesis 2-4. Likewise the need to limit the life and potential of man is consistent with the curses imposed in the fall narrative of Genesis 3 and the Cain episode of Genesis 4. Furthermore, the duration of human life in Genesis 6:1-4 differs from that reflected in the genealogies of Genesis 5 and Genesis 11.[5]

5. On Genesis 6:1-4 see especially B. S. Childs, *Myth and Reality in the Old Testament* (London:SCM Press, 1960), pp. 49-57.

Two Introductions to the Flood Stories

One of the conclusions to which many readers come as they study Genesis 6–9 is that there seem to be two different stories about the flood which are intertwined in these chapters. Even if we grant that a harmonizing process would naturally occur as these chapters were retold over the years, or that an editor organized these materials into an artistic unit, is there sufficient evidence remaining in the text to substantiate this frequent impression of two story lines? And if there are two such strands, are they related to the two groupings of material in Genesis 1–5?

We noted above that major structural divisions in Genesis are introduced by the expression, "These are the generations of, . . ." This formula normally marks a new phase in the divine plan of salvation history throughout Genesis. Genesis 6:9 begins with the same introductory formula. An appropriate introduction to the flood account appears in the following verses (Gen. 6:9–11). However, a parallel introduction had already preceded in Genesis 6:5–8 where the same basic points were made, but from a different orientation. The contrasting elements of these two introductions offer some of the most cogent arguments in favor of two distinct authors of the flood narrative.

In verses 5–8 the problem which God faces is the evil of man. This evil exists because of the "evil" in the "heart" of man. Employing rather a bold anthropomorphism the writer maintains that Yahweh "changed his mind" (*naham*) about the creation of man. Yahweh then deliberates with himself about "blotting out" (*mahah*) man from "the face of the ground." The resolution of man's fate lies solely in the grace of God. Noah "found grace!" Noah is not yet depicted as a hero of superior character. Thus the basic perspective of these verses seems to be consistent with that of the so-called Yahwist text in Genesis 2–4.

In Genesis 6:9–11 the introductory formula announcing the generations of Noah leads the reader directly to Noah as a great example of faithfulness, a hero who is both righteous and "perfect" (*tamim*). He, like his grandfather Enoch (Gen. 5:24), "walked with God." The situation which God must rectify in Genesis 6:9–11, however, is not primarily the evil of man as such, but the universal corruption at large in the earth. The earth is said to be "corrupt" (*shahat*) and filled with "violence" (*hamas*). Both of these Hebrew expressions suggest a chaotic force of destruction at work in the order

29

of creation. The perspective seems to be cosmic. Man as such is not the primary concern here as he is in Genesis 6:5–8. The blame is not laid directly on man as it is in the first introduction. Rather, the viewpoint of this introduction is in harmony with that expressed by the so-called Priestly Writer of Genesis 1.

The contrast between the two introductions to the flood narrative (A. Gen. 6:5–8; B. Gen. 6:9–13) can be seen by tabulating the major features as follows:

Introductory formula:	A. B. These are the *generations* of . . .
Divine recognition of the situation:	A. And *Yahweh* saw that . . . B. And *Elohim* saw . . . and behold . . .
Nature of the problem:	A. The *evil* in *man's* heart B. The *corruption* of the *earth*
Extent of the problem:	A. *Man's heart* and thoughts are evil continuously and totally B. Violence in the *earth* Corruption of *all flesh*
The reaction of God:	A. His heart is *grieved* *Changes his mind* about man B. God issues a decree to Noah
The verdict of God:	A. To obliterate *life* from the *ground* B. To destroy *all flesh* and *the earth*
Noah's role:	A. The chosen son of *grace* (cf. Gen. 7:1) B. The hero who is *perfect* in his day
Distinctive terms:	A. evil, obliterate, find grace, change one's mind, grieve in the heart, from the face of the ground B. violence, corrupt, destroy, his generation, the generations of . . ., perfect
Style:	A. Presented as an episode in which Yahweh sees, suffers, changes his mind, makes a decision, and gives grace. Colorful and dramatic. B. A formal introduction to Noah, his family, and the situation. God observes the scene and decrees. Repetitious and stiff. The action and decree of God (v. 13) repeats the wording of the previously described situation (in vv. 11–12).

Two Versions of the Flood Story

In Genesis 6:13–22 the divine instructions to Noah are formally delineated in great detail. "Two animals" from "all flesh" must be led into the ark. These must be "male and female" each "after its kind." God's intention to "destroy" all flesh is repeated (Gen. 6:13, 17) in the same formal terms as in the introduction of Genesis 6:9–12. God's relationship to Noah is defined in terms of a covenant. "I will *establish* my covenant with you" (Gen. 6:18) reappears as a central theological idiom later in Genesis. Noah executes God's demands "precisely as God commands" and thereby exhibits his character as a heroic example of unquestioning obedience.

In Genesis 7, however, God's instructions on how to load the ark are repeated. This set of directions seems to ignore the commands already given in Genesis 6:13–22. Noah is again introduced as a righteous man, that is, a man living in the right relationship with his God. He is thereupon commanded to take *seven* of each kind of animal into the ark. This time the animals are designated "man and woman" (or "a male and his mate"). God reiterates the purpose which he announced in the first introduction (Gen. 6:5–8), namely, to "obliterate" life "from the face of the ground." This devastation is to be achieved by sending rain on the land for forty days and forty nights. It seems therefore, that Genesis 7:1–5 presents a continuation of the first introduction in Genesis 6:5–8 and reflects the same perspective, while Genesis 6:14–22 perpetuates the features and thought of the second introduction in Genesis 6:9–13.

After Genesis 7:5 the two strands of the narrative are not as readily divided, or rather, the divergent materials do not fall into the neat blocks typical of the texts we have studied thus far. However, a reading of the two proposed sources as they have been translated in the following pages suggests the presence of two sets of materials, each of which presents a generally consistent portrait. This translation and division is given here for didactic purposes. We recognize that this kind of neat isolation of sources is not possible with the degree of accuracy which might be assumed by this translation. The retelling of the story, the transmission of the text, and the process of harmonization all argue against demanding the kind of precision in literary analysis which was presumed possible in the last century.[6] In short, the text of the following translation is designed to be illustrative rather than definitive. The distinctive and characteristic terms and expressions of each literary strand have been italicized so that the reader can observe some of the evidence for identifying one source or the other on literary grounds. This identification process also demands a consideration of the total perspective of the author involved in each case, a factor which can only be isolated by even closer scrutiny of each text in its context.

THE YAHWIST VERSION	THE PRIESTLY WRITER'S VERSION
(Gen. 6:5–8; 7:1–5, 7–8, 10, 12, 16b–17, 22–23; 8:2b–3, 6–12, 13b, 20–22)	(Gen. 6:9–13, 14–22: 7:6, 9, 11, 13–16a, 18–21, 24; 8:1–2a, 4–5, 13a, 14–17; 9:1–19)
Introduction (6:5–8)	*Introduction* (6:9–13)
[5]And *Yahweh* saw that the *wickedness* of man was great in the earth, and that every imagination of the *thoughts of his heart* was only *wicked* continually. [6]And *Yahweh was sorry* that he had made man on the earth, and *his heart grieved.* [7]So *Yahweh* said, "I will *blot out* man whom I have created from upon *the face of the ground,* man and beast, creeping things and birds of the air, because *I am sorry* that I made them." [8]But Noah *found grace in the eyes of Yahweh.*	[9]*These are the generations of Noah.* Noah was a righteous man, *perfect* among his contemporaries. And Noah *walked with God.* [10]And Noah had three sons, Shem, Ham, and Japheth. [11]And the earth grew *corrupt* before *God.* And the earth was full of *violence.* [12]And *God* saw the earth and behold it was *corrupt,* for all flesh had *corrupted* its way on the earth. [13]And *God* said to Noah, "I have determined to make an end of *all flesh,* for the earth is filled with *violence* through them and behold I will annihilate *(corrupt)* them *with* the earth."
Concerning the Ark (7:1–5)	*Concerning the Ark* (6:14–22)
[1]So *Yahweh* said to Noah, "Go aboard the ark, you and all your household, for I have seen that you are righteous before me in this generation. [2]Take with you *seven* pairs of all *clean* animals, *the male and his mate,* and one pair of the animals that are not	[14]"Make yourself an ark of resinous wood. Make it with reeds and cover it with pitch inside and out. [15]This is how you are to make it: the length of the ark 300 cubits, its breadth 50 cubits and its height 30 cubits. [16]Make a roof for the ark and finish it

6. One of the important efforts to modify the source analysis of the flood narrative on the principles of oral tradition studies is found in E. Nielsen's work, *Oral Tradition* (Naperville, Ill.: Allenson, 1954), pp. 93–103.

clean, *the male and his mate.* ³(Also from the birds of the heaven seven pair, male and female), to keep their seed alive upon *the face of* the earth. ⁴For in seven days time I will *cause it to rain* upon the earth *40 days and 40 nights,* and I will *blot out* everything *animated* which I made, from *the face of the ground.* ⁵So Noah did just as Yahweh had commanded him.

to a cubit above, and set the door of the ark in its side; make it with the first, second and third decks. ¹⁷For my part, behold I am bringing the flood of waters upon the earth to annihilate *(corrupt) all flesh* in which is the breath of life under heaven. ¹⁸But *I will establish my covenant* with you, and you shall go on board the ark, you, your sons, your wife, and your sons' wives along with you. ¹⁹And from every living thing of *all flesh, two of each sort* you shall bring aboard the ark, to save their lives with yours; they must be *male and female.* ²⁰From the birds according to their kind, from every creeping thing of the ground *according to its kind,* two of every sort shall come in to you to keep them alive. ²¹And take with you every sort of food which is eaten and store it up, and it shall serve *for food* for you and them. ²²So Noah did just as *God* had commanded him. *So he did.*

The Advent of the Flood
(7:7-8, 10, 12, 16b)

⁷Then Noah and his sons and his wife boarded the ark to escape the waters of the flood. ⁸From the *clean* animals and animals that are *not clean,* and from the birds, and from everything that creeps on the ground (they boarded). ¹⁰After *seven* days the waters of the flood came upon the earth. ¹²And *rain* fell upon the earth *40 days and 40 nights.*¹⁶ᵇ and Yahweh shut him (Noah) in.

The Advent of the Flood
(7:6, 9, 11, 13-16a)

⁶And Noah was *600 years old* when the flood of waters came upon the earth. (⁹Two of each kind boarded the ark with Noah, *male and female,* as *God* had commanded Noah.)

¹¹In the *600th year* of Noah's life, in the 2nd month, on the *17th* day of the month, *on the very day,* all the fountains of the *great deep* burst forth and the windows of heaven were opened. . . . ¹³On the very same day Noah and his sons, Shem, Ham and Japheth, and Noah's wife and the three wives of his sons with them, boarded the ark,

33

[14]they and every beast *according to its kind* and all the cattle *according to their kinds,* and everything that creeps on the earth *according to its kind,* and every bird *according to its kind,* every bird of every sort. [15]They boarded the ark with Noah, *two and two of all flesh* in which there was the breath of life. [16]And those who boarded, *male and female* from *all flesh,* entered as *God* had commanded him.

The Flood (7:17, 22-23)

[17]And there was a flood on the earth for *40* days. And the waters increased and lifted the ark and it rose above the earth. [22]Everything on the dry land in whose nostrils were the *breath of life* died. [23]He *blotted out* everything *animated* which was on the *face of the ground,* both man and beast, creeping things and birds of the heaven. They were *blotted out* from the earth. Only Noah was left and those that were with him in the ark.

The Flood (7:18-21, 24)

[18]The waters *prevailed* and increased *greatly,* and the ark went upon the face of the waters. [19]And the waters *prevailed exceedingly* upon the earth and covered *all* the high mountains which are under *all* the heavens. [20]The waters *prevailed* above the mountains, covering them fifteen cubits deep. [21]And *all flesh expired* that moved on the earth, birds, cattle, beasts, all *swarming creatures who swarm* on the earth, and every man. [24]And the waters *prevailed* upon the earth *150 days.*

The End of the Flood
(8:2b-3, 6-12, 13b)

[2b] Then the rain was restrained from heaven. [3a] And the waters receded from the earth continually. [6a] And at the end of *40 days* Noah opened the window of the ark which he had made. [7]And he sent forth a raven; and it went to and fro until the waters were dried up from the earth. [8]Then he sent forth a dove from him, to see if the waters had *subsided* from the face of the ground. [9]But the dove found no *resting place* for her foot, so she returned to him into the ark, for the waters were

The End of the Flood
(8:1-2a, 4-5, 13a, 14-19)

[1]Then *God remembered* Noah and all the beasts and all the cattle that were with him in the ark. And *God* made a wind blow on the earth, and the waters *subsided.* [2a]And *the fountains of the deep* and the windows of heaven were closed. [3b]At the end of *150 days* the waters had *abated.* [4]And in the 7th month, on the *17th day* of the month the ark came to rest on the mountains of Ararat. [5]And the waters continued to abate until the *10th month;* and in the *10th month,* the *1st day*

34

still upon *the face of* all the earth. And he stretched forth his hand and took her and brought her into the ark with him. [10]He waited another *seven days* and again he sent forth the dove out of the ark. [11]And the dove came back to him in the evening, and lo, in her mouth a freshly plucked olive branch. So Noah knew the waters had subsided from the earth. [12]Then he waited another *seven days* and sent forth the dove and she did not return to him any more. [13b]So Noah removed the covering of the ark, and looked and behold *the face of the ground* was dry.

of the month, the tops of the mountains were seen. [13a]In the *601st year*, in the *1st month*, on the *1st day* of the month, the waters were dried up from the earth. [14]In the *2nd month*, on the *27th day* of the month, the earth was dry. [15]*And God* ordered Noah: [16]"Go out from the ark, you and your wife, and your sons and your sons' wives with you. [17]Bring forth with you every living thing that is with you of *all flesh*—birds and animals and *every creeping thing that creeps* on the earth—that they may *breed abundantly* and be *fruitful and multiply* on the earth." [18]So Noah went forth, and his sons and his wife and his sons' wives with him. [19]And every beast, every creeping thing, and every bird, everything that moves upon the earth, went forth by families out of the ark.

Conclusion (8:20-22)

[20]Then Noah built an altar to *Yahweh* and took from every *clean animal* and every *clean bird* and offered burnt offerings on the altar. [21]When *Yahweh smelled* the pleasing odor *Yahweh said in his heart*, "I will never again *curse the ground* because of man for the *imagination of man's heart* is *wicked* from his youth. And I will never again smite all living creatures. [22]While the earth endures, seedtime and harvest, cold and heat, summer and winter, day and night, shall not cease."

Conclusion (9:1-17)

[1]*And God blessed Noah* and his sons, and said to them, "*Be fruitful and multiply,* and fill the earth. [2]The fear of you and the dread of you shall be upon every bird of the air, upon everything that creeps on the ground and all the flesh of the sea; into your hand they are delivered. [3]Every moving thing that lives shall be food for you; and as I gave you the green plants, I give you everything. [4]Only you shall not eat flesh with its life, that is, its blood. [5]For your lifeblood I will surely require a reckoning; of every beast I will require it and of man; of every man's brother I will require the life of man. [6]Whoever sheds the blood of man, by man shall his blood be shed; for *God* made man *in his own image.* [7]And you *be fruit-*

35

ful and multiply, bring forth abundantly on the earth and multiply in it."

[8]Then *God* said to Noah and to his sons with him, [9]"Behold, *I establish my covenant* with you and your *descendants after you,* [10]and with every living creature that is with you, the birds, the cattle, and every beast of the earth with you, as many as came out of the ark. [11]*I establish my covenant with you,* that never again shall *all flesh* be cut off by the waters of a flood, and never again shall there be a flood to destroy the earth." [12]And God said, "This is *the sign of the covenant* which I make between you and me and every living creature that is with you, for all future generations: [13]I set my bow in the cloud, and it shall be a *sign of the covenant* between me and the earth. [14]When I bring clouds over the earth and the bow is seen in the clouds, [15]*I will remember my covenant* which is between you and me and every living creature of all flesh; and the waters shall never again become a flood to *destroy all flesh.* [16]When the bow is in the clouds, I will look upon it and *remember the everlasting covenant* between *God* and every living creature of all flesh that is upon the earth." [17]God said to Noah, "*This is the sign of the covenant which I have established between me and all flesh that is upon the earth.*"

A careful scrutiny of the two proposed versions of the flood narrative above reveals an almost unbroken story line for both versions, despite the fact that these sources have been combined into one account. Each story has a theological introduction and conclusion giving divine reasons for the flood and divine reactions to it. Each version has its own rendering of the major elements of the story. And each rendering has its own consistent set of terms to describe the details of the flood story. This literary contrast is coupled with a theological contrast. The same conflicting theological approach discussed above in the introduction to the flood account persists throughout the narrative versions. Rather than discussing each of the literary and theological characteristics of each of these versions in detail, we have summarized the evidence in the following table. This evidence suggests that the two proposed literary sources or complexes isolated in Genesis 1–5 are continued in the two flood versions given above.

THE YAHWIST VERSION	THE PRIESTLY WRITER'S VERSION
Introduction: As in Genesis 2–4, *Yahweh* is portrayed in human terms. He suffers because of man. Man is his central concern. Man is to be removed from the ground. One man finds undeserved favor.	As in Genesis 1 *Elohim* stands at a distance and speaks decrees about the earth. Cosmic destruction is decreed upon the cosmic corruption. One man is found perfect.
The Divine Instructions: Noah is to take 7 of each of the clean animals into an ark and 2 each of the unclean.	Noah is to build an ark and take 2 of each kind of animal into the ark.
The Nature of the Flood: Yahweh sends rain (showers) which produce a flood capable of lifting the ark off the ground.	A cosmic upheaval occurs in which the cosmic waters above the heavens and the waters of the cosmic deep below the earth effect a return to chaos (as in Gen. 1:2). The mountains disappear.
The Duration of the Flood: Rain and flooding for 40 days and 40 nights. Noah waits three weeks before disembarking.	A full cycle of 12 months (or 1 year and 10 days) passes before creation is restored to order.
Conclusion: Yahweh is again viewed in human terms, smelling the sacrifice, talking to himself and expressing a promise never to smite life with a similar curse.	Genesis 9:1–17 offers a twofold conclusion, the first part reaffirming man's role as God's ruler on earth (vv. 1–7) and the second establishing a covenant between Himself and all Life.
Distinctive Expressions: wicked, blot out, face of the ground, find grace, subside, clean, be sorry, male and his mate, Yahweh, etc.	generations, corrupt, all flesh, expire, the deep, establish a covenant, the very same day, prevailed, according to its kind, swarming creatures who swarm, etc.

37

In addition to recognizing these literary features of the two flood versions, we can discern evidence of the literary structure of the Priestly Writer. We noted above how the Priestly Writer organized both the creation account of Genesis 1 and the genealogy of Genesis 5. His organization of the flood materials is calendric.

Genealogical Introduction:
6:9–10 "These are the generations of. . . ."

Calendric and chronological superstructure
to the events of the flood:

7:6	"Noah was 600 years old when. . . ."
7:11	"In the 600th year in the 2nd month. . . ."
7:24	"The waters prevailed 150 days. . . ."
8:3	"At the end of 150 days. . . ."
8:4	"In the 7th month. . . ."
8:5	"In the 10th month. . . ."
8:13	"In the 601st year. . . ."
8:14	"In the second month. . . ."

Genealogical Conclusion:
9:28–29 "After the flood Noah lived 350 years . . . and he died."

It is important to note that the events of the flood take twelve months[7] according to this pattern and that the whole episode is viewed as a restoration of the order of creation. In the ancient Near Eastern world the conflict between the forces of creation and chaos was thought to involve an annual battle, the victory of the God of creation being celebrated at the New Year festival. In this flood account dry land also appears on New Year's Day (Gen. 8:13) as a sign of new life and of God's control. However, the covenant by God in Genesis 9:8–17 asserts that there is no annual battle to be feared, but that God has the authority never to let the chaos waters return.

Two Conclusions to the Flood Narrative

The stylistic and theological similarities between the two flood accounts and their respective counterparts in the text

7. The Hebrew text has 12 months and 10 days, allowing for the 10 day intercalation adjustment between solar and lunar calendar, while the Greek translation (in the Septuagint) has precisely 12 months.

of Genesis 1–5 suggest the likelihood of two authors or organizers of material. The accumulated evidence seems to point specifically to the work of two men or schools of men who have arranged and colored the materials they have received for a specific purpose. The narratives are told, introduced, and presented to speak a pertinent message with a definite theological emphasis. This point can be argued, not only on the basis of how the events of the narrative are told, but also because of the structural organization of the materials in one complex (the Priestly Writer). These arguments are supported by the distinctive theological introductions and conclusions to the accounts of the flood. The introductions were discussed in some detail above. If our theory of two literary authors is plausible, the same kind of evidence for a distinctive perspective and purpose on the part of the respective writers should also be evident in their conclusions to the flood story.

The first conclusion in Genesis 8:20–22 incorporates a number of the same idioms and expressions found in the Yahwist version of the flood. The portrait of Yahweh, moreover, is totally consistent with the human way he is depicted in Genesis 2–4 and 6:5–8. Yahweh "smells" the odor of the sacrifice of Noah and "talks to himself" as he reacts to the changed situation after the flood. The problem of man's evil heart is the same as that presented in Genesis 6:5–8. Man remains the primary concern of this writer. The flood is described as a "cursing" of the "ground" (*'adamah*) because of man (*'adam*). The same terminology and motifs are found in Genesis 3:17, an earlier Yahwist section. The basis for Yahweh's decision never again to smite man or life on earth is the perpetual evil of man's heart. That reason is identical with the one given for sending the flood in Genesis 6:5–8. In short, the conclusion of the flood account by this author is a necessary complement to the introduction of Genesis 6:5–8 and consistent with the suggested Yahwist materials in Genesis 1–8.

The conclusion of the second author is somewhat longer (Gen. 9:1–17). Some of the typical expressions which suggest the hand of the Priestly Writer in this text include, "And God blessed . . . and said . . . ," "be fruitful and multiply," "fill the earth," "for food," "image," "establish my covenant," "all flesh," "eternal covenant," and the like. Genesis 9:1–6 continues the theme of man as God's vice-regent, operating in God's image, and controlling the earth. This perpetuates the motif and language of the Priestly Writer in Genesis 1:26–28 and 5:1–3. The new features introduced include an element of fear which makes man's task of controlling earth more difficult, and the right of man to kill animals provided their blood is not consumed. In Genesis 9:7–17 Elohim issues his decree and promise that no more floods will appear on earth. No ground for his decree is given (as it is in Gen. 8:21). His promise, moreover, is not made only with man, but with all of nature, and a cosmic sign is set in the heavens to remind Elohim of his own promise. The concept of the covenant as "eternal," as "established," and as a promise "with you and your descendants after you" is found many times throughout Genesis in later materials of the Priestly Writer.

Conclusions

Our preceding analysis of Genesis 1–9 suggests that certain kinds of literary evidence can be isolated. In some sections this evidence is more obvious than in others. The evidence was sought both in generally parallel accounts of a common subject and also in the combined account of one tradition. We have proposed that where the evidence for a given style occurs, a specific set of literary idioms and terms is consistently present. Each combination of style and terminology is supported by a corresponding literary or theological outlook. The combined "constants" of style, terminology, and perspective provide the primary evidence for maintaining that two literary sources are present in Genesis 1–9. To this evidence we would add the above indications of structural organization and arrangement of the literary materials.

We recognize that each of the two literary sources or complexes involved are dependent upon earlier materials, whether literary or oral. The two literary sources under consideration in Genesis 1–9 are not so much sources as interpretations and formulations of earlier traditions. It is our contention that literary evidence can isolate two such formulations of past traditions available to the ancient Israelite writer. In some cases the smaller units incorporated by the writer may be modified very little, if at all. Examples of this may be seen in the cry of Lamech at the end of the Yahwist genealogy (Gen. 4:23–24), or the blessings and curses at the end of the flood narrative (Gen. 9:25–27). The presence of such relatively independent units within the total complex does not nullify the literary evidence cited above. These units do, however, force us to recognize the limited nature and extent of the literary process involved.[8]

Nor is it possible to be dogmatic about the precise division of literary sources in many combined accounts. Our division of source materials in the flood narrative was illustrative rather than definitive. We must grant the possibility of conflated stories being combined in an oral stage as well as the probability of later literary editors removing inconsistencies or difficulties in the text. The repeated copying and use of literary materials would also tend to soften the differences between one original literary hand and another. Examples of this may perhaps be found in the flood narrative. The unexpected use of the Priestly Writer's favorite term "create" in the Yahwist introduction to the flood in Genesis 6:7 may be explained on these grounds. A similar difficulty is presented by the appearance of the Priestly Writer's terminology in Genesis 7:3a and 9, verses which appear within larger blocks of Yahwist material. More important, however, is the fact that so much evidence of distinct literary sources or writers has been preserved and has not been obliterated by later redactors.

We must also view this literary evidence in terms of the writer who compiled Genesis 1-9. Whoever this writer was, he did not attempt to unify style, terminology, and perspective so as to remove the tensions and differences that existed. It is quite possible that the writer in question was the Priestly Writer. His tendency to provide structures and frameworks for his materials support his candidacy for literary organizer of the materials of Genesis 1-9. The significant fact remains, however, that he did not attempt to eliminate duplicate features. Two introductions and two conclusions stand as testimonies to two differing approaches to the

8. Space does not permit an answer to past criticisms of the source hypothesis of the Pentateuch. Many of these are directed against a form of literary critical analysis which does not take into account form criticism or tradition studies, or against that kind of literary critical process which claims to be able to divide verses with an unwarranted degree of finality. In other cases the attack is directed against the evolutionary approach to religion which Wellhausen supposedly espoused and reflected in his interpretation of the literary sources of the Pentateuch. The current understanding of the literary critical process is not linked to this approach, but takes into account all the recognized techniques of historical critical research. Typical negative analysis of the source hypothesis of the Pentateuch include U. Cassuto, *The Documentary Hypothesis* (Jerusalem: The Magnes Press, 1961) and E. Young, *An Introduction to the Old Testament* (Grand Rapids: Eerdmans, 1958).

41

flood narrative. He apparently honored the theology of his sources. If he is the organizer and final interpreter of Genesis 1–9, we may have a clue as to why he did not include in his own hand anything about the fall of man or the death of Abel.

The preceding analysis does enable us to assert some kind of major literary continuity within two different groups of material traditionally identified with the work of the Yahwist and the Priestly Writer. Many elements of these two literary sequences gain special significance in the light of literary and theological connections after Genesis 9. The Sabbath and the covenant concepts are features of the broader superstructure of the Priestly Writer. For the Yahwist the struggle between Yahweh and Cain has significance in the light of subsequent Yahwist encounters between man and God. The following chapters will attempt to underscore the continuity of purpose and character in each of these two literary sources. For the Yahwist and the Priestly Writer are more than literary artists or organizers of accumulated traditions. They are theological interpreters of their people's history. It is this dimension of the sources of the Pentateuch to which we shall also address ourselves in the subsequent chapters.

In summary, we can assert that the preceding literary evidence apparent in Genesis 1–9 suggests the probability of two literary complexes or writers. The dependency of these complexes on prior traditions, oral forms, or literary units is in no way challenged by this conclusion. On the basis of these considerations we shall proceed to investigate the literary and theological character of two of the major literary sources of the Pentateuch so as to gain a richer appreciation of the literary critical process when applied to the Pentateuch.

III

Interpreting Literary Sources: The Yahwist and the Promise

As a literary artist the Yahwist[1] has been compared to Homer and as a theologian to St. Paul. These accolades may be true but they may also prove a smoke screen for the beginning student of the Pentateuch. He wants to see the evidence for a Yahwist source beyond the texts of Genesis 2-9. We could, of course, follow the lead of most introductions to the source hypothesis of the Pentateuch and list all proposed Yahwist style and theology. Such a method is comfortable. It adopts the findings of some great scholar and assumes that the evidence for identifying the Yahwist writer throughout, the Pentateuch is the same or similar to that provided in the preceding analysis of Genesis 1-9. The critical reader, however, will want to test these assumptions. He will want to know what kind of data, criteria, or evidence play a role in the identification and understanding of the Yahwist in the patriarchal, exodus, and wilderness traditions.

It is obvious that we will not have opportunity here to discuss each proposed Yahwist passage. Nor will we have a chance to treat many passages where the separation of Yahwist and Elohist sources is problematical. We shall therefore choose typical and normative materials to illustrate the literary character of the Yahwist subsequent to Genesis 2-9. In so doing we hope that convincing connections with the Yahwist texts of Genesis 2-9 will become apparent and the governing characteristics of the Yahwist's total literary work will be revealed. At the same time we do not want the bold outline of the Yahwist which follows to obscure the fact that many contours of the Yahwist literary source have become blurred in the course of textual redaction and transmission.

THE YAHWIST AT WORK: A CLASSIC PASSAGE

Genesis 18 provides a profitable example of Yahwist literary formulation. In this chapter we can discern many of

1. The writer of the Yahwist literary source is usually designated the Yahwist as though he were a clearly identifiable individual. For the sake of convenience we have preserved this traditional designation. See P. Ellis, *The Yahwist* (Notre Dame, Ind.: Fides Publishers, 1968) for a recent analysis of Yahwist style and theology. This book provides a complete text of the Yahwist.

those features which are normative and typical of his literary artistry. A brief analysis of the chapter points up the following structural outline.

18:1-15 The Theophany at Mamre
  a. The Meal (1-8)
  b. The Annunciation (9-15)
	(A) A patriarchal tradition story with editorial marks

18:16-21 The Decisions of Yahweh
  a. Moving to Sodom (16)
  b. Soliloquy One (17-19)
  c. Soliloquy Two (20-21)
	(B) A transition text with programmatic Yahwist passages

18:22-33 The Dialogue over Sodom
  a. Introduction (22)
  b. The Dialogue (23-32)
  c. Conclusion (33)
	(C) A patriarchal tradition of heroic intercession

The three kinds of literary material suggested by the above outline provide suitable general categories for studying much of the Yahwist's literary work. To the first category belongs that mass of patriarchal traditions which have been preserved and formulated by the Yahwist in concise and classic story form. In this connection scholars have praised the grace, simplicity, economy of words, rapid movement of events, the suggestion of a setting with but limited detail, the building of suspense and the ability to involve the reader in the drama of an episode, as features typical of this master storyteller. Much of this honor may be due to ancient bards and elders of Israel who retold these incidents in the community circle. Be that as it may, many of these traditions have been preserved, reformulated, introduced, and combined by someone into a literary whole. Marks of one literary artist, identified here as the Yahwist, reappear within the text and context of these classic stories.

What are the grounds for that assertion? Let us consider first the literary features of Genesis 18:1-15. Legends about men entertaining divine beings or the annunciation of special births by heavenly figures can be found elsewhere in ancient literature. But few compare with this one in irony, simplicity, and beauty. Three men appear before Abraham in the heat of the day. The very hour of their appearance suggests something unusual about the adventure. Mystery shrouds the en-

44

tire scene. The men are not identified to Abraham and their purpose is not revealed until after the meal. Abraham must first play the hospitality game. The account of that game is a masterpiece of humor and style. Each action is reported with extreme brevity and each statement is an ironic understatement. Abraham depicts himself as the supremely unworthy host. Typical Yahwist expressions which highlight that feature in the speeches of Abraham include, "your *servant*," "if I have found *grace*," "a *little* water," and "a *morsel* of bread."

By contrast, the actions of Abraham betray his intense efforts to please his guests with a massive display of hospitality. It is the heat of the day and yet every move of Abraham denotes great exertion. He "*runs* to meet" his unexpected, unidentified guests. "He *bows* to the earth" and "*washes* their feet." He "*hastens* to the tent" and orders cakes to be "made ready *quickly*." He "*runs* to the field," "*takes* a calf," and has his servant "*hasten* to prepare it." After this frenzy of activity on behalf of his alien guests he steps aside in silence as they conclude their veritable banquet of veal, curds, milk, and fresh cakes.

After the meal, the first remark of the satisfied guests has the potential to shock even the most congenial host in the ancient Near East. They bluntly ask for Abraham's wife. The gasping listener is quickly assured that their purpose in coming is honorable if indeed ridiculous. What man would be interested in Sarah, that laughing old woman eavesdropping from within the goatskin tent? Then suddenly the mood switches. The hospitality game is followed by a divine joke. The guests announce a miracle. Barren old Sarah is to have a baby boy by the following Spring. That was too much too soon for Sarah. She laughs her head off and reveals her unfaith. In so doing she establishes the character and name of her future son as Isaac, the Joke, the Laughing One. He is to be the miracle child whose coming was announced by the passing strangers at the banquet in the heat of the day.

How does the Yahwist betray his hand? Apart from the subtleties and word colors of the story already mentioned and specific expressions such as "find grace in your eyes," we can recognize an editorial framework. The story as such relates the advent of three men to Abraham's tent. Their names are unknown to Abraham. In his editorial preface, however, the Yahwist interprets the story of their coming as a theophany. He explains that God "appeared" to Abra-

45

ham (v. 1). The Yahwist, moreover, identifies that God as "Yahweh," the God of Israel. Likewise in verse 13 he identifies the previously anonymous spokesman of the three as Yahweh. In short, we see signs of an author retelling and interpreting this ancient patriarchal tradition in terms of his faith in "Yahweh's" guidance of patriarchal history. This observation is supported by the connected segment of material in Genesis 18:16–21. To this text we shall turn our attention below.

Many other patriarchal stories are preserved by the Yahwist with minimal editorial change. Typical examples include the jeopardizing of Abraham's beautiful wife (Gen. 12:10–20), the destruction of Sodom (Gen. 19:1–28), the discovery of Rebekah and the betrothal of Isaac (Gen. 24:1–67), and the blessing of Isaac (Gen. 27:1–45).[2]

The second major literary unit of Genesis 18 consists of verses 16–21. This unit, in turn, has three relatively independent sections (v. 16, vv. 17–19, and vv. 20–21). The first of these (v. 16) is a unifying passage designed to link the preceding theophany episode with the following record of Abraham's intercession for Sodom. The same function is served by verse 22. These two verses introduce the Sodom setting and the opportunity for Abraham to confront Yahweh with an alternate solution. Verses 20–21 go a step further and provide the divine rationale for the forthcoming destruction of Sodom. This rationale is given in the form of a divine soliloquy and corresponds to the divine musings in passages such as Genesis 6:7; 8:21–22; or 11:6–7. In typical Yahwist style Yahweh is the speaker and the reader is the listener. Yahweh is heard speaking to himself about the latest problem that has arisen on earth. As on other occasions Yahweh is portrayed in blatantly human terms. He has to check out the situation at Sodom to determine its seriousness. Then he will "know." As at the tower of Babel, Yahweh sighs, "Let me go down and take a look. . . ." It is in these soliloquies and similar passages where we find the Yahwist giving an explicit interpretation of Yahweh's role and character as he directs the course of history. They offer Yahweh's rationale for his own action. These texts, as in Genesis 18, are usually supplementary to the story line of the context but are given to interpret, introduce, or reflect upon the episode involved. Among the list of these rationale passages we

2. See also Genesis 38:1–30; Exodus 2:1–10; 2:11–22; Numbers 12:1–16 and 24:4–59.

should mention Genesis 2:18; 3:22; 6:5–8; 8:21–22; 11:6–7; 18:20–21.

The divine soliloquy of Genesis 18:17–19 is equally important. Its significance lies in its programmatic character. Yahweh's words' are not á command to Abraham concerning a specific situation in the life of the patriarch. His divine self-deliberation is not part of the story line of the episodes that precede or follow. Rather these words interpret what Yahweh was "up to" in the total life of Abraham. They give the divine program for the destiny of the patriarchs. Through this soliloquy the writer interprets what Yahweh was doing. Precisely because this is a programmatic passage we meet a set of loaded terms that reflect the theological perspective of the Yahwist. Verse 17 expressly asserts that Yahweh has a plan for the seed of Abraham. The nature of his destiny is summarized in the great Yahwist expressions clustered together in verse 18: "a great and mighty nation," "by him they will be blessed," "all nations of the earth."

Variations of these thematic expressions occur in other programmatic passages, but not with sufficient consistency to argue for a second literary hand in these texts. These programmatic texts provide the basis for our study of how the Yahwist develops his interpretation of the patriarchal promise. All of these passages have Yahweh speaking to himself or to a hero. Usually they are cast in the form of a promise. The passages involved include a sequence relating to the future of Abraham (Gen. 12:1–3; 13:14–17; 15:4–5; 18:17–19; 26:2–5; 28:13–15) and a similar sequence pertaining to the promised land (Gen. 12:7; 15:18–21; Exod. 3:7–8, 16–17). Many of the thematic terms from these programmatic passages appear as earmarks of Yahwist interpretation in other contexts as well. As examples we might cite Genesis 24:7; 27:27–29; 30:27; Numbers 22:6 and 24:9.

The third major literary unit of Genesis 18 is the dialogue over Sodom (vv. 22–33). Dialogues are not unusual in themselves, but when we meet God and man locked in this kind of bold verbal duel we sense something special. In the Pentateuch that kind of encounter reflects the mood and message of the Yahwist. Apart from the Yahwist connection in verses 16–21, the dialogue is introduced with Yahweh standing before Abraham in a typical human stance of subservience. (The RSV at this point preserves the later version of the text according to which Abraham stands before Yahweh). The dialogue itself enables Abraham to be the hero, the mighty mediator. He makes a valiant effort to save despicable Sodom. He appeals for justice to Yahweh, "the judge of all the earth." Ultimately his demand is dependent on more than justice. Only on the basis of mercy could Yahweh spare that city and on that score Abraham, Jacob, and Moses appeal for deliverance again and again. They are portrayed as the great heroes of the promise. The language of this dialogue reflects that kind of bold epic encounter. "Far be it from you," cried Abraham. Or in a modern translation he cries, "How dare you? Surely the Judge of all the earth will do the decent thing" (v. 25). Abraham cajoles God down from fifty to ten potential redeemers within the city. But the city apparently has no righteous inhabitants. As in the story of the flood they all deserve to die. Lot alone finds grace.

Similar dialogues appear throughout the Yahwist materials of the Pentateuch. In most cases we feel the same direct fearless encounter with the deity. There is something epic and mighty in the way these men of God grapple with their Lord. They are giants of prayer and intercession. Their God is so accessible he almost seems vulnerable.

THE NEED FOR THE PROMISE

Our analysis of Genesis 18 was more than an exercise in literary skill. Here we saw the Yahwist at work as an interpreter in one segment of Genesis. Literary cirticism is also concerned with tracing the hand of this interpreter wherever he may be found. In so doing we can discover one way in which the ancient traditions of Israel were understood by its spokesmen. How does the Yahwist treat his traditions? What fresh insights into Israel's past are gained by tracing his interpretations through the Pentateuch? What do we unveil if we follow the trail of his programmatic passages and comments from Abraham to Moses? The outline of the Yahwist source which follows does not claim to cover all of the major themes or techniques of its author. We shall focus upon the motifs of programmatic texts such as Genesis 18:17–19 treated above. This means that the promises to the patriarchs will be at the core of our investigation. We shall discuss their function in the literary plan of the Yahwist. Thus we shall highlight their importance for a rich understanding of this literary strand in the Pentateuch. We hope thereby to illustrate further how the results of literary criticism aid the student of the Pentateuch.

Genesis 12:1–3 stands at the head of the patriarchal history and sets the agenda for the program of salvation.[3] In the wording of the Yahwist, Yahweh outlines a plan of blessing for the patriarchs, their seed, and their neighbors. The governing thematic terms are italicized in the following translation.

Now *Yahweh* said to Abram:
"Go from your country and your kindred
and from your father's house
to the *land* that I will show you.
And I will *make you a great nation*
and I will *bless you*,
and I will *make your name great*
so that you will be *a blessing*.
And I will *bless* those who bless you;
and those whom you curse I will *curse*.
*By you all families of the ground
will be blessed*."

This plan of blessing begins with the patriarchs. It is absent from the primeval history. In fact the term "blessing" plays no important role in the Yahwist texts of Genesis 2–11. He views the primeval era as the age of man under the curse. With Genesis 12:1–3 a new way of blessing is opened for one family and its contacts. Genesis 2–11 shows the need for that new plan of salvation. His unique portrait of the background and need for these promises commences with Genesis 2, which is programmatic for the Yahwist's understanding of man.

The Yahwist begins by establishing an intimate bond between Yahweh and man (*'adam*) on the one hand, and between man and the ground (*'adamah*) on the other. Yahweh molds man and gives him life. Man is animated dust and Yahweh is his personal master (Gen. 2:4b–7). Man's tie with the earth is also expressed in his character as a farmer. Before his advent there was no man (*'adam*) to till the ground (*'adamah*). After his creation Yahweh plants a garden for man to till and keep. Yahweh, in turn, cares for man and experiments with various forms of life to find a suitable companion for man. Like man, all the animals are formed from the ground. A special creative act was required, however, to produce a partner fitting for man (Gen. 2:8–25). The symbol of Yahweh's authority is found in the form of a tree called the tree of the knowledge of good and evil. Thus the stage is set for the progress of primeval history.

3. Perhaps the best treatment of the promise texts of the Yahwist is that of Hans Walter Wolff, "The Kerygma of the Yahwist," *Interpretation* 20 (1966): 131-58.

The Yahwist narratives in Genesis 3–11 follow a general pattern of sin, judgment, and grace or sin, punishment, and forgiveness. This pattern is evident in the Adam, Cain, Noah, and Babel stories. In each case sin disturbs the balance between Yahweh, man, and the ground. The first humans rebel by eating from the forbidden tree. The crime of Cain is murder in the first degree. At the time of the flood, evil is rampant in the hearts and lives of all men. The tower of Babel episode portrays man challenging Yahweh in heaven above. In these accounts the Yahwist portrays man as a powerful rebel. He has surging evil drives that must be controlled by one means or another. From the beginning man chose a course in opposition to Yahweh and in conflict with his fellowman. Adam and Cain are characteristic of all men.

In his preface to the flood story the Yahwist defines the nature of man (Gen. 6:5–8). His heart is so corrupt that all of his ideas are evil. This utter perversity of man is the basis for Yahweh's decision to exterminate all men. Because man is apparently trapped in this condition Yahweh discards annihilation as a future solution (Gen. 8:21). Yahweh's answer to the uprising of mankind at Babel was dispersion by confusion of languages. Here again the abnormal potential of evil man is emphasized. "Nothing that they propose to do will now be impossible for them" (Gen. 11:6). A similar limitation of human control is reflected in the soliloquy of Genesis 3:22 where Yahweh decides to expel man from the garden because "he has become like the gods, knowing good and evil." According to the Yahwist, man has the drive to conquer the heavens and partake of the divine. That urge must be kept within bounds. "Hence," says Yahweh, "my spirit will not abide in man *forever*, for he is flesh" (Gen. 6:3). There must be a limit to man's life span. As Yahweh faces man's growing potential for evil he sets new limits to his capacity. The patriarchs are men of like character. They are heirs of these primeval rebels and in need of divine deliverance. Accordingly the Yahwist portrays the patriarchs in their full human colors.

The judgment phase of the Yahwist pattern of primeval history is regularly defined in terms of the curse. After the fall, the snake is cursed by Yahweh and destined to eat dust (Gen. 3:14). The ground (*'adamah*) is cursed because of man (*'adam*). In the sweat of his brow he must till that ground until he returns to the dust from which he came (Gen. 3:17–

19). Thus the eternal link between man and the ground is reaffirmed. The curse expresses the alienation of man from that ground. The curse is evoked by man but the ground suffers as a result. Cain too is "cursed from the ground" when Yahweh hears the blood of Abel crying from that ground (Gen. 4:10–11). This enmity persists between Cain and the ground. It will never yield to Cain's hand (Gen. 4:12).

With the flood story Yahweh's judgment reaches extreme proportions. He plans a universal curse. Man is to be exterminated "from the face of the ground" (Gen. 6:7; 7:23). For Noah's son Canaan the curse meant a history of abject slavery. "Cursed be Canaan, a slave of slaves he shall be to his brothers" (Gen. 9:25). Dispersion is the course of action taken at Babel; man is scattered abroad "across the face of all the earth" (Gen. 11:8–9). Like Cain he is forced to wander and his powers are curtailed. Hence, at the brink of the patriarchal age we find man spread over the accursed ground. Man has failed to achieve a great name for himself (Gen. 11:4). The future of man under the curse is a vast question mark.

Punishment by Yahweh is normally followed by expressions of his grace and forgiveness. The very survival of Adam is evidence of divine forbearance. Yahweh did not execute his threat of capital punishment. There is life for man despite the curse. Adam names his wife Eve because she is "the mother of all living" (Gen. 3:20). Further, Yahweh fashions clothing for the first couple. This act symbolizes the divine acceptance of man regardless of his sin and disgrace (Gen. 3:21). Cain, too, is given a sign of Yahweh's grace. The mark he receives assures him of protection while wandering through the earth (Gen. 4:13–16). Even this murderer is not put to death. Despite his deed, he confronts Yahweh with a blunt protest, "I cannot stand this punishment." This bold appeal of Cain wins mercy. He is protected even though he deserves death. In this he becomes a hero. The Yahwist includes many such heroes. They are men under the curse whose audacity gains them Yahweh's goodwill. Man is not impotent before the curse. He can scream to Yahweh for a revised plan of action.

It is typical of the Yahwist that Yahweh can and will change his mind. The decision of Yahweh to annihilate man means that his "experiment" with mankind has apparently failed. "He changed his mind about making man" (Gen. 6:7). That decision, in turn, is reversed by divine grace. "Noah found grace in the eyes of Yahweh" (Gen. 6:8). The decision, however, is not a fickle change of mind. He "grieved" over the condition of man before the flood (Gen. 8:6) and he rejoiced with Noah after the flood (Gen. 8:21). The welfare of man demands that Yahweh never again "curse the ground because of man" nor disrupt the cycles of nature (Gen. 8:21-22). Man can only survive if Yahweh operates on the grounds of free and forthright grace.

The sudden dispersion of mankind after the Babel episode leaves the world inhabited by a mass of frustrated rebels who have thwarted Yahweh's kindness at every turn. But with the advent of Abraham we hear the good news of a fresh program of redemptive action announced by Yahweh himself (Gen. 12:1-3). The sweeping array of promises wrapped in a concise message to Abraham offer Yahweh's personal dramatic answer to the looming question about God's goodwill to all men scattered across the "face of the ground." Now "all families of that ground will be blessed through Abraham," whispers Yahweh (Gen. 12:1-3). By Abraham the curse which was rampant over the ground during primeval times will be reversed and a bold new plan of blessing set in motion. As we trace this bundle of promises through the Pentateuch we shall be demonstrating a concern for more than literary style. Terminological features will inevitably be involved in the analytical process and certain identifying features will continue to be underscored, but thematic and programmatic characteristics will also be given due attention. For the theological perspective and groundwork uncovered in our study of Genesis 2-11 must now be related to the major centralizing motif of the promise to Abraham. Can that motif be isolated as a literary thread of the Yahwist? Does it persist as a governing theme in the midst of a vast panorama of old stories that seem to capture the interest of the reader on their own terms? Can a literary analysis discern those features of the record which reveal the Yahwist as an interpreter as well as a brilliant storyteller?

THE PATRIARCHS AND THE PROMISE

Genesis 12:1-3 appears to be both the structural climax to the fourfold cycle of sin, judgment, and grace developed in the primeval history and also the *magna carta* for the fresh plan of redemption extended to the patriarchs. In the chapters which follow Genesis 12:1-3 the Yahwist is especially interested in how these promises fare at the hands of doubting and devious men like the patriarchs. Hence the Yahwist's selection of patriarchal narratives seems to be related to the fate of the promise given to Abraham in Genesis 12:1-3 and subsequently reiterated in various forms. The patriarchal stories illustrate the numerous obstacles that stood in the way of accepting the promise and the extreme lengths to which Yahweh went in order to fulfill the promise. Interpretive comment and promise formulation within the narrative accounts indicate how the Yahwist links his stories and relates them to the governing motif of his work. The central unifying elements of the programmatic passages are drawn together in the text of Genesis 12:1-3. These themes can be summarized under four heads: seed, land, greatness, and mediation of blessing.

Seed: those chosen descendants who heard and transmitted the promises through the era of doubtful beginnings to the day of expansion and nationhood.

Land: that territory of Canaan and beyond which Yahweh bound himself by covenant to give to Abraham's seed as their inheritance.

Greatness: the destiny of Abraham's sons to achieve a great name and nationhood, despite the repeated possibility of their annihilation.

Mediators of Blessing: the privilege and responsibility of Abraham's seed to mediate the blessing of life to neighboring nations.

The bundle of promises in Genesis 12:1-3 is also a direct call for Abraham to express his faith in Yahweh by leaving his homeland and wandering off to some unknown corner of the earth. This initial outburst of faith is immediately tested when Abraham discovers that the promised land is really controlled by Israel's ancient enemy. Indeed, comments the Yahwist, "the Canaanites were then in the land" (Gen. 12:6). As we will come to expect in Yahwist contexts, the pertinent promise is repeated when its potential fulfillment has been challenged. "To your seed I will give *this land*" cries Yahweh. Canaan is not for the Canaanites, but for Abraham's progeny.

Time and again the promise stands in jeopardy. The sequence of narratives which the Yahwist selects for Genesis accentuates this precarious pose of Yahweh's good news to the patriarchs. For hardly has the promise been announced and confirmed upon arrival in Canaan when Abraham's land and seed are both in danger of becoming lost dreams. A famine arises in Canaan and Abraham runs to the nearest prosperous civilization for aid (Gen. 12:10–20). His lack of trust is further exhibited when he thinks of his own neck and allows Sarah to become Pharaoh's wife. Only by drastic divine intervention is Abraham rescued and his wife restored unharmed. Curse rather than blessing is mediated to the Egyptians as plagues fall on Pharaoh's household and foreshadow greater plagues to come.

Despite his spectacular deliverance from Egypt, Abraham must live with Canaanites and with a brother (Lot) who grabs the choicest regions of the land (Gen. 13:1–18). This situation prompts the Yahwist to add a postlude addressed to Abraham that heightens the previous promises of territory and progeny:

All the *land* which you see I will give *to you* and to *your seed* forever. I will make *your seed* as *the dust* of the earth, so that if one can count the dust of the earth, *your seed* also can be counted (Gen. 13:14–16).

Abraham's need for a son is the focal point for several episodes selected by the Yahwist interpreter. Abraham doubts whether any natural course of procreation will provide him with an heir. He therefore tries to guarantee progeny by proposing that he follow the ancient Near Eastern custom of adopting a slave as one's heir (Gen. 15:1–6). Yahweh immediately rejects this scheme of Abraham and counters with a clear repetition of the promise that a son from Abraham's own loins will be his heir. The closing comment of the Yahwist at this point expresses succinctly his whole theological attitude to the patriarchal promise and its function in the life of those men. "Abraham believed in Yahweh and Yahweh counted that faith to him as righteousness" (Gen. 15:6). His living faith in the face of unbelievable odds establishes a true relationship with Yahweh. No cultic or sacrificial act was necessary to gain public recognition as a righteous man before God.[4] Faith in Yahweh and his prom-

4. Note especially G. von Rad, "Faith Reckoned as Righteousness," in *The Problem of the Hexateuch and Other Essays* (New York: McGraw-Hill, 1966) for a complete discussion of this text.

ise was the crucial ingredient that bound Abraham to his God. This dilemma of faith continues to be posed by the Yahwist as generation after generation confront Yahweh and his good news.

Even the doubts of Abraham persist. "O Yahweh God, how am I to know that I shall possess it (the land)," he retorts (Gen. 15:8). Yahweh's complete commitment to his promise of the new land is publicized by an ancient covenant rite (Gen. 15:7-21). Here only do we find the Yahwist linking the patriarchal promise to an explicit covenant. He reports that, "Yahweh cut a covenant with Abraham saying, 'To your seed I will give this land, from the river of Egypt to the great river, the river Euphrates'" (Gen. 15:18). The extent of this projected empire suggests the greatness of the Davidic domain.[5] Those who were flushed by the sudden advent of power, greatness, fame, and international influence under David and Solomon certainly needed to hear the message that all their might was an undeserved gift and all their blessings due to Yahweh's patient guidance of his promised plan. Neither Israel nor their patriarchal forefathers had done anything along the way to earn that kind of goodness and glory.

The machinations of Abraham lead him to devise another means of obtaining progeny by begetting children through his concubine Hagar (Gen. 16:1b-2, 4-14). His scheme backfires, however, when Sarah forces the woman and her child out into the wilderness. Ironically Hagar is protected and given the divine blessing because of her association with Abraham. Thus Abraham unwittingly mediates blessing to the Ishmaelites, the descendants of Hagar's son Ishmael. Barren and disbelieving Sarah remains the final great obstacle to any possible fulfillment of Yahweh's promise for seed from Abraham's loins. She laughs with disdain at the announcement of her forthcoming pregnancy. The prediction of the three mysterious messengers from the desert is no more than a joke to her (Gen. 18:1-15). As analyzed earlier, this narrative is followed by a programmatic passage outlining Yahweh's intentions for Abraham. Once again the reason for the promised miraculous birth is the ultimate goal

5. R. Clements in *Abraham and David* (London: SCM Press, 1967) has isolated royal terminology in Genesis 15 and thereby introduced additional evidence for linking the chapter with the Davidic era. We should also make it clear that there is considerable difference of opinion among critics on the extent of the Yahwist material in this chapter. A variety of factors in the transmission of the traditions has no doubt led to a blurring of the original literary source contours.

of greatness and mediated blessing which Yahweh plans to effect through the seed of Abraham. The soliloquy of Yahweh makes this conclusion clear:

Then *Yahweh* said, "Shall I hide from Abraham what I am about to do, seeing that Abraham shall become *a great and mighty nation,* and that *by him all nations of the earth shall be blessed?* For I have *chosen* (known) him, that he may charge his children and his household after him to keep the way of Yahweh by doing righteousness and justice; so that Yahweh may bring to Abraham what he has promised him" (Gen. 18:17–19).

The following heroic dialogue between Yahweh and Abraham suggests a further explication of Abraham's role as a mediator of blessing. He attempts to salvage Sodom by a direct appeal to Yahweh (Gen. 18:22–33). The account of the destruction of Sodom is somewhat similar to the flood narratives (Gen. 19:1–38), for this account functions as an illustration of the continuing evil of man in need of Abraham's blessing and the ultimate judgment that descends when evil reaches unbearable proportions. The cry had reached heaven and Yahweh was moved to action (Gen. 18:20). As in the Noah tradition, the household of Lot survives the holocaust by the grace of God. His family, too, believes they are the last surviving people on the earth.

Into that evil world the promised son is born. Yahweh overcomes all the obstacles set by Abraham or his household and visits Sarah with a miracle (Gen. 21:1–2). "Who would have said to Abraham that Sarah would suckle children?" she cries (Gen. 21:6–7). With this dramatic beginning the promise is finally on the road to fulfillment. This seed is not a part of the natural order of things implanted in man at the beginning (as in Gen. 1:28). Isaac represents a new line that arises in the face of old, impotent, and doubting parents. The child is a gift of grace, a seed of hope, and a sign of the promise. Such is the perspective of the Yahwist program of salvation through promise. The Yahwist expansion of the story of the attempted sacrifice of Isaac underscores this governing viewpoint (Gen. 22:15–18).[6]

As the Yahwist interprets the course of patriarchal history, the line of Isaac has to be kept intact and kept pure. Isaac is not to select a wife "from the daughters of the Canaanites" among whom Abraham dwelt (Gen. 23:3). The story of the courtship of Rebekah illustrates this motif and highlights

6. The story of Isaac's near sacrifice is usually assigned to the Elohist, although this is far from certain. In any case the appendix to the story in Genesis 22:15–18 bears the marks of a Yahwist reinterpretation.

several others (Gen. 24:1 67). Foremost among these is the theme of greatness for Abraham and his progeny. Abraham has been blessed and his servant is certain that the God of Abraham will prosper his way. The extent of Abraham's might is related by the servant to the household of Laban:

I am Abraham's servant. Yahweh has greatly *blessed* my master, and *he has become great*; he has given him flocks and herds, silver and gold, menservants and maidservants, camels and asses (Gen. 24:34–35).

Wealth is the first expression of that greatness. A second element is enunciated by the relatives who bless Rebekah with the words, "Our sister, be the mother of thousands and tens of thousands, and may your seed possess the gate of those who hate them" (Gen. 24:60).

The greatness of Abraham is surpassed by the wealth of Isaac. His prosperity is achieved at the hands of the Philistines despite his own folly in surrendering his wife to Abimelech (Gen. 26:1–33). This achievement of Isaac at Philistine expense anticipates the later role played by David. The blessing of Isaac is described in Yahwist terms:

Isaac sowed in the land and reaped in the same year a hundredfold. Yahweh *blessed him* and the man *became great*. And *he became even greater* until he *became very great*. He had possessions of flocks and herds and a large household so that the Philistines envied him (Gen. 26:12–14).

This account of the jeopardizing of Rebekah and the subsequent prosperity of Isaac is preceded by a lengthy introduction in Genesis 26:2–5. These verses are not integral to the story itself but provide the Yahwist's continuity between the promise to Abraham and the first of his seed. The past promise to Abraham is now defined as an oath that must be kept by Yahweh. The consistent dimensions of the promise are reflected in the recurring terminology:

Sojourn in this land of which I shall tell you. I will be with you and bless you; for *to you* and *to your seed* I will give all these lands, and I will fulfill *the oath* which I swore to Abraham your father. I will multiply *your seed* as *the stars* of heaven, and I will give to *your seed* all these lands. And *by your seed all nations of the earth shall bless themselves* (Gen. 26:3–4).

The promise to Abraham is viewed as normative for his descendants. They gain salvation because of the oath sworn to Abraham and are blessed "for my servant Abraham's sake" (Gen. 26:24).

The oath to Abraham is threatened by the antics of Jacob. The Yahwist exposes Jacob as a scoundrel who usurps the blessing and takes advantage of its power. Like his father Isaac, Jacob is a miracle child born from a barren mother (Gen. 25:21-26). Through Yahweh's special answer the promise of seed is preserved. Jacob's character, however, is hardly appropriate for Yahweh's chosen line. He tricks Esau into gaining birthright privileges from his brother (Gen. 25:27-34), and he schemes with his mother to obtain the filial blessing of Isaac (Gen. 27:1-45). That blessing turns out to be a poetic version of the patriarchal promise of greatness that suggests the might of David's empire:

May God giv you the dew of heaven and of the fatness of the earth, and plenty of grain and wine. Let *peoples* serve you and *nations* bow down to you. Be lord over your brothers and may your mother's sons bow down to you. *Cursed be every one who curses you and blessed be every one who blesses you* (Gen. 27:28-29).

The stolen blessing from Isaac is confirmed by the promise of blessing from Yahweh himself (Gen 28:13-16). This passage is the Yahwist's programmatic text introducing the life of Jacob. The promise is connected with his journey away from the promised land, just as the initial promise to Abraham was linked to his trip from Mesopotamia and the opening promise to Isaac was tied to his journey into Philistine regions. In this promise to Jacob, great progeny and the mediating of blessing are closely related to the immediate assurance of inheriting the land. The continuity between this promise and its predecessors is reflected in Yahweh's self-identification as the God of both Abraham and Isaac. The dispersion of Jacob's seed in all directions is designed to provide blessing for all nations of the earth. This promise naturally recalls the expansion of the Davidic empire and suggests the divine reversal of Yahweh's earlier curse on all peoples when he scattered them in all directions (Gen. 11:1-9). This promise given to Jacob is worded as follows:

I am Yahweh, the God of Abraham your father and the God of Isaac; the land on which you lie I will give *to you and to your seed*; and *your seed* shall be like *the dust* of the earth, and you shall spread abroad to the west and to the east and to the north and to the south; and *by you and your seed shall all families of the ground be blessed.* Behold I am with you and will keep you wherever you go, and will bring you back to this ground, for I will not leave you until I have done that of which I have spoken to you (Gen. 28:13-15).

The narrative cycle relating to Jacob and Laban seems to include at least two different traditions (Gen. 29–31). The editorial hand of the Yahwist, however, is clearly evident. Not only does Jacob gain a large family, but he is blessed at every turn. He cannot help prospering (Gen. 30:30). More significantly, this blessing is mediated to Laban. "I have learned by divination," states Laban, "that Yahweh has *blessed me because of you*" (Gen. 30:27). And Jacob confesses that, "If the God of my father, the God of Abraham and the Fear of Isaac, had not been on my side, surely now you would have sent me away empty-handed" (Gen. 31:42).

The narratives about Jacob's return from Haran and his confrontation with Esau are again interpreted in the light of the promise. Jacob's prayer for help is worded in terms of Yahwist theology. Jacob admits he was blessed by the undeserved grace of Yahweh and recognizes his two companies as the result of divine goodness. His demand for future deliverance, however, is not based on any vow of loyalty, any oath of allegiance to God's law, any commitment of homage, but upon Yahweh's past promise of numerous seed. To Yahweh's face he cries, "*You yourself said*, 'I will do you good, and make your seed as the sand of the sea, which cannot be numbered for multitude'" (Gen. 32:12). That promise is the ground of Jacob's violent appeal. His is a heroic demand matched only by his nocturnal struggle for a special blessing (Gen. 32:24–32). The greatness of Jacob lies in these bold encounters with Yahweh from whom he wins protection, blessing, and a new name. His name Israel expresses that greatness, "for," says the angel of the night, "you have striven with God and men and have prevailed" (Gen. 32:28).

The cycle of stories related to Joseph and the descent of Jacob's household into Egypt highlights the mediating of blessing to Egypt in the face of apparent disaster for Israel (Gen. 39–47). Immediately upon arrival in Egypt the Yahwist declares that "Yahweh blessed the Egyptian's house for Joseph's sake; the blessing of Yahweh was upon all he had, in house and field" (Gen. 39:5). Even in prison Joseph continues in favor with both Yahweh and his prison keeper. His activity in prison is prospered by Yahweh himself. Nothing could stop the power of his blessing. His good fortune and political power are divine schemes to rescue his own family from starvation. Once in Egypt the household of Jacob again prospers until the Egyptians cry, "Behold the people of Israel are too many and too powerful for us" (Exod. 1:9). The Yahwist concludes the development of the patriarchal blessing motif in Genesis by incorporating Jacob's blessings for each of his twelve sons (Gen. 49:1–28). In this sequence the promise of ultimate political greatness and national might is given to Judah. He is to inherit the scepter and the obedience of the peoples (Gen. 49:8–12). In this blessing it seems that the Yahwist is deliberately linking the promise to the patriarchs with a later fulfillment under the Davidic monarchy. Through David the tribe of Judah gained "the scepter" of kingship and became a nation capable of ruling other peoples. With poetic beauty this final patriarchal promise reads:

> The scepter shall not depart from Judah,
> nor the ruler's staff from between his feet,
> until he comes to whom it belongs;
> and to him shall the obedience of the peoples be (Gen. 49:10).

MOSES AND THE PROMISE

The patriarchal promise motif does not die with the patriarchs. Granted it does not appear with the same frequency or with the same full complement of terminological identification marks as in Genesis, but the basic promise theme remains a driving impulse for motivating Yahweh's actions. Many new colors and concepts now arise in the Yahwist portraits of Israel's history, but at crucial scenes in the life of Moses' people the promise reappears as the word of deliverance or the salutary basis for appeal. A demonstration of how this governing motif operates in the Mosaic period is attempted here as we quickly trace several normative Yahwist catchwords and concepts through Exodus and Numbers.

Throughout the Mosaic era we find deliverance evoked by heroic pleas of intercession, public cries of agony, or direct prayers of mediation. The endless scream of Israel under Egyptian bondage is the first great appeal that moves Yahweh to keep his promise (Exod. 3:7–8). As on past occasions the Yahwist describes Yahweh "coming down" to get personally involved in the human struggle (cf. Gen. 11:7). His goal is to deliver Israel from Egypt and return his people to their land, the land of the Canaanites. In the words of the Yahwist, the Lord is acclaimed as "Yahweh, the God of your fathers, the God of Abraham, of Isaac and of Jacob" (Exod. 3:16). Yahweh is identified by virtue of his association with the heroes of the promise, and he renews that ancient promise of land to his oppressed people in slavery

(Exod. 3:16–17). In this connection Moses becomes the peculiar symbol of Yahweh's mercy and the mediator of his promised program. "They will not *believe* me," objects Moses (Exod. 4:1). Like their forefathers the Israelites are not ready to "believe" without the assurance of signs and wonders (Exod. 4:1–31). At the crossing of the Red Sea the Israelites finally come to trust Yahweh and his representative. Only then do they "see the great work which Yahweh did against the Egyptians," and "*believe* in Yahweh and in his servant Moses" (Exod. 14:31).

The obstacles to fulfilling Yahweh's promises experienced by the patriarchs are dwarfed by the catastrophe of Israel's slavery. Deliverance called for drastic measures. And while the Yahwist includes the many plagues imposed upon Egypt to effect deliverance, he still sees opportunitites for mediating forgiveness and blessing even to the oppressor. "Forgive my sin, I pray you, only this once, and entreat Yahweh your God only to remove this death from me," pleads Pharaoh to Moses and Aaron (Exod. 10:17). After the Passover Pharaoh grants permission for Israel to worship for three days in the wilderness. At this time he is heard to summon Moses, "Go serve Yahweh your God, as you have said. Take your flocks and your herds, as you have said, and be gone, *and bless me also*" (Exod. 12:29–32). Pharaoh, too, seems to want the blessing available through the line of Abraham. Thus it is that Israel leaves Egypt, having "*found grace* in the eyes of the Egyptians," and having expanded to a "mixed multitude" (Exod. 12:33–39).

Throughout the wilderness travels Moses is portrayed as the mediator of life for the sons of Israel. Through direct communication with Yahweh he can avert doom for his own people just as he could revoke the curses upon Egypt. Like the patriarchs before him, his word can evoke unequivocal divine grace because of the promise. When the Israelites murmur over conditions at Marah and Rephidim, Moses intercedes on their behalf and Yahweh provides a convenient solution to the problem (Exod. 15:22b–25a; 17:1–7). Moses not only represents the people before Yahweh, however, but he also mediates Yahweh's will to the people. The fate of Israel depends on believing Moses, the mediator. The great theophany of Yahweh at Sinai (Exod. 19:9–25) is therefore designed to arouse trust in Yahweh and in Moses his spokesman:

And Yahweh said unto Moses, "Lo, I am coming to you in a thick cloud, that the people may hear when I speak *with you,* and may also *believe you forever* (Exod. 19:9).

According to the Yahwist, Moses and Joshua ascend the mountain to receive the two tables of stone (Exod. 24:12–15a). Before descending they are confronted by Yahweh with an ultimatum for disaster. The golden calf built by God's people at the foot of the mountain is viewed by God as an enormity comparable to the evil of Sodom. It means death for Abraham's family line and a chance for Moses to inherit the promised blessings of progeny and great nationhood. It means an end to the old plan and the beginning of a new. It means starting another experiment, this time with Moses as the projected great nation:

Now therefore let me alone that my wrath may burn hot against them; but *you I will make a great nation* (Exod. 32:10).

Moses' response to the tirade and decision of Yahweh reflects the themes and theology of the Yahwist's work evident in the patriarchal stories. The grace of Yahweh is won by the bold word of a hero. The ground is Yahweh's own promise, for on that basis he can change his mind about the annihilation of his people. The classic protest of Moses recalls explicitly the oath to Abraham, Isaac, and Jacob. The promise is indeed Israel's means of survival.

Moses *entreated Yahweh* his God and said, "O Yahweh, why does your wrath burn hot against your people, whom you have brought forth from the land of Egypt with great power and with a mighty hand? Why should the Egyptians say, 'With *evil intent* he brought them forth to slay them in the mountains and consume them *from the face of the ground?'* Turn from your fierce wrath and *change your mind concerning this evil* against your people. Remember *Abraham, Isaac and Israel* your servants to whom *you swore* by your self and said to them, 'I will multiply *your seed* as *the stars* of heaven and all *this land* that I have promised I will give to your seed, and they shall inherit it forever.'"

So *Yahweh changed his mind* concerning *the evil* he planned to do to his people (Exod. 32:11–14).

A series of crisis situations arise after this dramatic act of deliverance at Sinai that reflect a similar pattern of salvation by intercession typical of Yahwist thinking.[7] These crises culminate in Israel's cowardice before the giants of Canaan. Once again Yahweh chides his people for disbelief, and

7. See Numbers 11:1–3; 12:1–16; 11:7–15 (especially v. 15); 11:16–19 and 11:31–35.

threatens to reorganize the program of promise around Moses by making him a great nation. Israel is not to inherit the promised land.

And Yahweh said to Moses, "How long will this people despise me? and how long will they not *believe in me*, in spite of all the signs I have wrought among them? I will strike them with pestilence and disinherit them, and I *will make of you a nation greater and mightier* than they" (Num. 14:11–12).

Moses thereupon takes up the cudgels for his people and bluntly confronts Yahweh with the situation. As Moses sees it, to disinherit Israel means that Yahweh will lose face in the sight of the other nations. Blessing cannot be mediated by annihilating the agents of blessing. Hence, Moses pleads for forgiveness and power from Yahweh commensurable with his past promises: "Let the power of Yahweh be as great as you have promised" (Num. 14:17). He asks for forgiveness on the ground that Yahweh has forgiven previously (Num. 14:13–19). The response of Yahweh is a modified expression of grace (Num. 14:20–25). As in previous instances the rebellion of man reaches a point where judgment is necessary. All but one of that generation of Abraham's seed would die before the land sworn to the fathers would be conquered and possessed. Caleb alone, like others before him, has a different spirit and finds grace in the eyes of Yahweh. The final great act of saving intercession by Moses is found in Numbers 21:4–9 where Yahweh instructs Moses to set up a bronze snake as a symbol of life to which all would turn in faith for healing.

Many of the Yahwist motifs are drawn together in the final series of texts dealing with Balaam. Moses' intercessions had rescued Israel time and again. Balaam's prayer now threatened to overthrow her. The Yahwist introduces Balaam as a professional expert in the art of cursing and blessing. He is summoned precisely because Israel had become a mighty nation and his curse is requested to counter the fulfilled blessing of Yahweh. "Come now curse this people for me," asks Balak, "since they are too mighty for me . . . I know that he whom you bless is blessed, and he whom you curse is cursed" (Num. 22:6). This wording recalls the promise of blessing and curse given to Abraham in Genesis 12:2–3. Balaam, however, is prevented from bringing a genuine curse upon Israel and ends up repeating an oracle of victory, prosperity, and blessing (Num. 24:3–9). This oracle reaffirms the past promises of Yahweh to the patriarchs and concludes with a recollection of Genesis 12:2:

Blessed is every one who blesses you
and cursed is every one who curses you (Num. 24:9).

A subsequent oracle focuses upon the conquest of all the neighboring nations of Israel at the hand of the "star of Jacob." This figure is probably to be identified as the house of David through whom the promise of a great Israelite nation is fulfilled in the mind of the Yahwist writer (Num. 24:15–24).

Whether the Yahwist text ends at this point is not clear. The Balaam oracles, however, do provide a fitting finale to the Yahwist portrait of the plan for the patriarchal promise. Israel has become a nation too powerful for Moab to handle (Num. 22:6). The promised land awaits Israel's invasion. A glorious and prosperous kingdom is envisioned for God's people (Num. 24:6–7). A plan of conquest through the "star of Jacob" is spelled out by Balaam (Num. 24:15–24). He also delineates the same program of mediated blessing or cursing to any who acknowledge or reject Israel respectively. All of this is by the grace of Yahweh. If Israel has any doubt about that truth they need only recall one other incident that happened at Baal Peor (Num. 25:1–5). For at the very last minute, with a land in their grasp and Yahweh's promises all but completely fulfilled, the Israelites again revert to disbelief. They worship Baal and indulge in the fertility orgies of the local shrine.

When the greatness of the Davidic empire was finally achieved, Israel was forced to admit that she did not deserve the land or the fulfilled promises. To the bitter end, the history of the promise is a history of sheer grace in the eyes of the Yahwist. With literary finesse, beauty, and polish that message is conveyed through colorful narrative form. And with strategically placed references to the governing promise motif, the Yahwist work illustrates a provocative ancient mode of interpreting Israel's past traditions. The forcefulness of these insights, we contend, can only be fully appreciated when the techniques of literary criticism employed above are rigidly applied.

IV
Interpreting Literary Sources: The Priestly Writer and the Covenant

The Priestly Writer has been called everything from a fastidious archivist to a cultic activist. Neither characterization is happy. Rather, he is a literary architect whose materials include history, theology, and liturgy. He is a designer who is more interested in symmetry than in storytelling. He favors continuity over color. He concentrates, above all, on where and how the God-given orders of life and salvation fit together. Hence he searches for patterns in the progression of God's activity from creation to Canaan. In so doing he uncovers a divine master plan that embraces a series of related orders, progressions, patterns, and structures. Some of these reflect the adaptation of existing forms, while others seem to be his own inspired discoveries. An example of the latter can be seen in his unveiling of the names of God. We mentioned earlier that the Yahwist used the name Yahweh for God even in the early chapters of Genesis. Seth calls upon the name of Yahweh (Gen. 4:26). The Priestly Writer, however, distinguishes three stages in the revealing of God's name. Each stage, it would seem, corresponds to a fixed period in the plan of redemption:

a. *Elohim* is the general name for God. This title alone is used by the Priestly Writer for the primeval period (Gen. 1:1 ff.).

b. *El Shaddai* is the first special name for God. This name is first revealed to the chosen patriarchs and is reserved for that era (Gen. 17:1 ff.).

c. *Yahweh* is the second special name for God. This name is first revealed to Moses and is never set in the mouth of any speaker prior to Moses (Exod. 6:2 ff.).

How does the preceding characterization of the Priestly Writing fare when we begin to analyze the texts after Genesis 1–9? Can the formal features of the so-called master plan of redemption be isolated? We contend that they can. And hence our first concern will be a study of the structural framework and features usually assigned to the hand of this writer. Since he is also a theologian, we may assume that he employs his literary structures for exhibiting his theological

65

program. Literary plan and theological perspective can hardly be divorced in such a work. At the heart of that plan the covenant with Abraham demands our attention and provides us with an excellent motif for special analysis. The reader can then compare the covenant theology of the Priestly Writer with the promise theology of the Yahwist treated in the previous chapter. Obviously we cannot investigate all of the Priestly Writing, but a survey of the structural elements and a closer consideration of the covenant theology should reveal the unique character of this literary source and the value of isolating its units for thematic analysis on their own terms.

THE PRIESTLY WRITER AT WORK

The Priestly Writer is a literary designer concerned about exposing the internal structure and arrangement of God's plan of creation, salvation, and sanctification. Everything has its place and explanation in that divine ordering of life. We noted earlier how the flood narrative was arranged according to a detailed calendric progression in which the dry land appears on New Year's Day. That timetable stands in contrast to the simple announcement of the Yahwist that Yahweh sent rain forty days and forty nights. The journeys of the Israelites from Egypt to Canaan are likewise organized in terms of a cultic calendar. Times, dates, numbers, ages, periods, and formal progressions are integral to the approach of this writer. Order is essential to his theology and his methodology. His patterns are not of one kind, however, and his three stages in the unveiling of God's name are but one contour of the divine master plan. Creation, history, and cult are all united in a sacred order revealed according to God's own timetable. In that order the continuity of mankind is carefully established by the Priestly Writer.

The movement of mankind from Adam to Aaron is unified by the introduction of generations or family histories (genealogies).[1] These link the beginnings of mankind with the patriarchs, the patriarchal heroes with the Israelites, and the Israelite people with their priesthood. The following table outlines that sequence of genealogies.

1. The generations of Adam	Gen. 5:1–32
2. The generations of Noah	Gen. 6:9–10

1. An adequate analysis of the genealogies in question can be found in a new work by M. D. Johnson, *The Purpose of the Biblical Genealogies* (New York: Cambridge University Press, 1969).

3. The generations of the sons of Noah   Gen. 10
4. The generations of Shem   Gen. 11:10-26
5. The generations of Terah   Gen. 11:27
6. The generations of Ishmael   Gen. 25:12-16
7. The generations of Isaac   Gen. 25:19-20
8. The generations of Esau   Gen. 36:1-43
9. The generations of Jacob   Gen. 37:1-2
10. The generations of Aaron   Num. 3:1-3
     (and Moses)

Each of these genealogical units is introduced with the technical term *toledot*, meaning generations or family history. Within this structure of ten genealogies additional patterns and numbers are repeated. Ten preflood heroes establish life on the earth in the first phase of human history. Between creation and chaos a full cycle of humanity lived upon the earth. The fullness of that cycle is represented in the number ten and corresponds to the ten postflood heroes (from Shem to Abram).

The Priestly Writer's use of the number ten is matched by his interest in families of three. Noah has three sons (Shem, Ham, and Japheth) who propagate the earth after the flood. Of these, the line of Shem is selected for God's covenant purposes. Terah has three sons (Abram, Nahor, and Haran) from whom all the patriarchs and their wives are chosen. The patriarchal stock is thus kept pure. From Abraham three family trees grow, those of Isaac, Ishmael, and Esau. These three lines continue to have close contact throughout Israel's early history. Of these three, Isaac's household is given the covenant promise for the future plan of God. Finally one figure from the twelve tribes of Jacob is elected as God's man for the priesthood. He is the culminating choice in a long line of divine selections as all the genealogies ultimately narrow down to Aaron, the last sacred hero. And he too has three sons (Nadab, Abihu, and Eliezer) who become the authorized fathers of all the legitimate priestly families. Generation after generation God chose key men to separate and sanctify for himself a peculiar people. In that sacred and salutary progression the guiding hand of the Priestly Writer is disclosed.

Another classic example of how the Priestly Writer orders his traditions can be seen in Numbers 1-10. With meticulous detail the tribes and priests of Israel are numbered by generations as they leave Sinai. Each priest or Levite is assigned

67

a specific sacred function and each tribe marches with identifying standards or ensigns. In this way the community is arranged according to a disciplined unity with the tent of meeting as the holy center. Each of the marching groups is arranged by families in relation to that sacred focal point. Each household must march in rank according to the order decreed as the tribes move through the wilderness by divinely designated stages. Nothing happens by chance, impulse, or common consent. A prior decree of God governs all movements. By that word a unified and sanctified people is created in accordance with God's timetable. Here the ideal people is that unique community, chosen by God, ordered by his decrees, moving forward at his command, and organized around his cultic center. Such an ideal reflects the harmony of God's original creative work.

The Priestly Writer seems to long for a return of that kind of worshiping community where God lives at the center and where life is programmed through the directives of his priests. Such a disciplined communion of people would be *tamim* (perfect), that is, whole and holy. Its members would be "perfect" like many of the great examples of faith praised in the genealogies. These genealogies unite Adam made in the image of God, Noah who was "perfect" in his generation, Abraham who walked before God to become "perfect," and all that obedient community made holy before the presence of God at Sinai. The genealogies, replete with sacred patterns and symbolic numbers, provide the sanctified thread unifying all of history. The true community is born of God's own selection as he directs the course of history from Adam to Aaron.

The Priestly Writer, however, is not content with these strands of genealogical continuity. He also wishes to demonstrate a correlation between the families of mankind and the natural orders of creation. To this end he adds a preface to his work which governs certain basic relationships that follow. The scheme of creation portrayed in that preface is also termed a genealogy. "These are the generations (genealogy) of the heavens and the earth," asserts the Writer (Gen. 2:4a). This genealogy, too, culminates in the sacred as the seventh day is separated and sanctified for God's blessing and rest. Thus there is built into the very order of creation a sacred seventh day. That day is the day prepared from the beginning for the later command to keep the Sabbath as a holy day. To observe the Sabbath, therefore, means to be in tune with creation.

The Priestly Writer, however, does not report the celebration of the Sabbath until it is divinely instituted as an official day of worship. Similarly no other sacred or cultic acts are performed by the heroes of Israel's past until they are actually announced by God himself at the appropriate time. No one anticipates the destined sequence of God's announcements, yet God himself prepares for his own decrees by his manner of structuring creation and history. Thus the seventh day of rest at creation becomes the Sabbath day at Sinai. There the Sabbath is hailed as a great covenant sign that unites Israel's experience of God at Sinai with his creative activity in the distant past (Exod. 31:13-17). Creation and salvation are embraced in one cultic sign, the Sabbath. Correlations of this kind are typical of the Priestly Writer's penchant for an integrated cultic order in creation and community.

The creation account of Genesis 1 is a masterpiece of structural balance and literary arrangement.[2] Certain features of this literary and theological design are immediately obvious. As noted earlier, the eternal creative decrees of God are ten in number. Ten times we read, "And Elohim said . . . ," and ten times new orders of creation were established. These ten words may simply reflect this writer's attachment to that sacred number, but they may also correspond to the ten words (later called Ten Commandments) given at Sinai, to order the lives of God's people. This ten-word design for the creation narrative is, however, a later superstructure imposed upon an underlying plan of eight acts in six days. This basic structural pattern of the six days of creation can be seen in the tabular outline below.

Stage One		Stage Two		
Light is created	1st day	corresponds to 4th day		Light-bearing bodies are made: sun, moon, stars.
A firmament separates the waters	2nd day	corresponds to 5th day		Life populates firmament and watters: birds and fish.
Dry land is made	3rd day 1st act	corresponds to day	6th 1st act	Life populates the dry land: animals.
Vegetation appears and multiplies	2nd act		2nd act	Man is made and vegetation is given to him as food.

2. See C. Westermann, *The Genesis Accounts of Creation* (Philadelphia: Fortress Press, 1964). A more complete study of the literary features of Genesis 1:1-2:4a suggests that an earlier literary pattern or structure lies behind the current Priestly organization of the material. A fine technical study has been done by W. Schmidt, *Die Schöpfungsgeschichte der Priesterschrift* (Neukirchen: Neukirchener Verlag, 1964).

This symphony of creation is perfected by a prelude and a postlude. The prelude of Genesis 1:1-2 describes the chaos and disorder existing before the creative work of God began.[3] The six-day plan of creation outlines the order brought to the universe and all of its living parts. The postlude corresponds to the prelude and highlights a seventh day when peace reigns and God rests. On that day the ordering of all creation is finalized and the stage set for man to participate in and enjoy that order through worship. Within the overall design of creation the creative works of the second, fourth and sixth days are classified as having governmental purposes. On the second day the firmament is established to preserve the cosmic order of the universe (Gen. 1:6). The dangerous waters of chaos are thereby kept at bay. On the fourth day the heavenly bodies are created to regulate calendric and cultic order (Gen. 1:14). They provide cosmic guides for signs, seasons, days, and years. On the final day man is placed upon the earth to govern all life as God's representative (Gen. 1:26). The complete ordering of life and the cosmos is thereby established for future generations. The Priestly Writer affirms the goodness of that order for the disciplined community of God's people, and he reflects that structuring of that divine work in the literary design of his text.

The creation plan of Genesis 1:1-2:4a is, moreover, integrated with the entire covenant progression of the Priestly Writer. A tabular demonstration of the Priestly Writer's outline should prove helpful at this point. Here the orders of creation, history, and cult are given new meaning and force by the addition of covenant promises and signs.

A. The First Order: Cosmic

a. Elohim establishes the orders of creation: the firmament guarantees cosmic order (Gen. 1)

a. Elohim establishes order after the flood: the chaos waters are again controlled (Gen. 8)

b. *Elohim* issues a *covenant* promise guaranteeing eternal cosmic order (Gen. 9)

c. A *covenant sign* is set in *nature* attesting the covenant: the rainbow (Gen. 9)

---

3. Formally the introduction to Genesis 1 is similar to those of the creation narratives in Genesis 2:4b ff., and the Enuma Elish of Babylon. See E. A. Speiser, *Genesis* (Garden City: Doubleday, 1964), pp. 8-13.

B. The Second Order: Human

a. Elohim establishes the original relationship between God and man: the image of God (Gen. 1:26–28)

a. A new relationship is established with Abraham: he is "perfect" before God (Gen. 17:1)

b. El Shaddai issues a covenant promise guaranteeing eternal force to that relationship (Gen. 17)

c. A covenant sign is set in man attesting that covenant: circumcision (Gen. 17)

C. The Third Order: Cultic

a. Elohim establishes one sacred period of rest and sanctifies it for his world: the seventh day (Gen. 2:1–3)

a. At Sinai a complete ordering of cultic periods, personnel and objects is decreed (Exod. 25–31)

b. Yahweh announces a covenant sign establishing his role as the one who sanctifies his people (Exod. 31:12–17)

c. The covenant sign of the Sabbath is set in the cult and is connected with both the covenant people and the order of creation (Exod. 31:12–17)

This broad outline of the Priestly Writer's perspective provides but a framework for considering his message. As already indicated, additional complex designs can be found throughout his work. Nevertheless, this progression underscores the basic plan and suggests the centrality of the Abraham covenant. This covenant is the moving force for the plan of salvation. The cultic order is ultimately dependent upon the covenant with Abraham, and through him with all God's people. Sinai organizes the covenant people, but it does not establish their relationship with Yahweh. That central covenant program initiated with Abraham and remembered with Moses is the source of hope and security for God's people. That aspect of the Priestly Writer's theology now demands our attention.

THE ABRAHAM COVENANT INITIATED

The Abraham covenant of Genesis 17 is preceded by the covenant with nature announced to Noah in Genesis 9. That chapter offers us a valuable introduction to the covenant style and language of the Priestly Writing. For the covenant of Genesis 9 is presented as a divine decree that establishes a binding relationship between God and his world in which

God alone makes the commitment.[4] The covenant is given continuity by designating the recipients as "you and your seed after you." Even more significant is the revelation that this covenant announces a new age which replaces the former precarious order of creation. The pertinent section of that divine proclamation reads:

> Behold I *establish my covenant* with you *and your seed after you,* and with every living creature that is with you, the birds, the cattle, and every beast of the earth with you, as many as came out of the ark. I will *establish my covenant* with you, that *never again* will *all flesh* be cut off by the waters of the flood and *never again* shall there be a flood to destroy the earth (Gen. 9:10–11).

The enduring worth and force of that covenant is underscored by recurrent expressions like "my" covenant, "eternal" covenant, "establish," and "remember." The covenant depends on God alone. He initiates it and imposes no conditions upon man or nature. The rainbow set in the heavens is God's own sign of his personal commitment to the promise he has made. Man can see that sign and be sure that God will "remember" and act in good faith. Or as the Priestly Writer words it:

> "When the *bow* is in the clouds, I will look upon it and *remember* the *eternal covenant* between me and every living creature of *all flesh* that is upon the earth." God said to Noah, "This is the *sign* of the covenant which I have *established* between me and *all flesh* that is upon the earth (Gen. 9:16–17).

This covenant language reflects the literary expression of the Priestly Writer's basic covenant orientation. Covenants are decrees of God that guarantee the ordering of one phase of life. They are eternally binding and their force is irrevocable. Covenants are born in the grace of God, filled with promises of security and formulated as divine pronouncements. An external sign may attest them, but the eternal word of God's command guarantees them. Man responds in wonder. His activities are not essential to the ultimate force of the covenant.

With some modifications the same covenant concept inheres in the Abraham covenant of Genesis 17. This chapter presents the agenda for the central covenant theology of the Priestly Writer. In that sense Genesis 17 is the Priestly counterpart to the Yahwist promises of Genesis 12:1–3 treated in

---

4. A convenient history of the covenant concept is given in the work of D. R. Hillers, *Covenant: The History of a Biblical Idea* (Baltimore: Johns Hopkins Press, 1969).

chapter three. The covenant pronouncements and promises of Genesis 17 are evident in the following sequence:

A. Announcement of the Covenant
   1a.   Editorial preface
   1b–2. Identification of El Shaddai and his intent
   3–8.   The promise of numerous seed for Abraham
           —the possession of Canaan as their heritage
           —a covenant with them as their God
   9–14. The sign of circumcision decreed
B. Announcement of a Son
   15–21. The promise of a son to Sarah
           The covenant to be established with the son
C. Response of Abraham
   22–27. Abraham fulfills the obligation of circumcision
           His whole household, including Ishmael, is circumcised

Here God (*Elohim*) reveals himself as *El Shaddai*, the great cosmic lord. The Priestly Writer reserves that distinctive name of God for covenant announcements connected with the patriarchal era (Gen. 17:1; 28:3; 35:11; 48:3). By translating this name God Almighty the RSV blurs the fact that *El Shaddai* is a definite name which differs from the general word for God (*Elohim*). God as the great creator dwelling on the cosmic mountain seems to capture the ancient meaning of that name. Abraham is summoned before this God and commanded to be "perfect." Like Noah before him (Gen. 6:9), Abraham is to be the epitome of obedience. This portrayal of the patriarchs as "perfect" is characteristic of the Priestly perspective. God commands and they obey. We find none of the foolish and sinful patriarchs of the Yahwist narratives. There is no hesitation in the faithful response of these great patriarchal examples when the Priestly Writer reports their actions. Thus, ". . . on the very same day Abraham did exactly as God commanded" (v. 23) and again, "that very day Abraham and his son Ishmael were circumcised . . ." (v. 26).

Abraham exhibits his exemplary attitude by ordering the immediate circumcision of his household. The Priestly Writer considers circumcision a sign that corresponds to the rainbow of the covenant with nature announced to Noah. The covenant concept remains essentially that of a one-sided divine commitment. The obligation of circumcision is the evidence of Abraham's response and involvement. By this once-in-a-lifetime deed Abraham binds himself to *El Shaddai*. Yet the sign of circumcision serves as a sacral identification mark and a continuous reminder of God's promise to his people rather than a law code. Historically it was in the exilic period that this identification symbol became especially meaningful.

Attendant upon the covenant in the Priestly Writer is a special promise of numerous seed. The Yahwist had treated this promise in terms of numerous seed that would culminate in a great and mighty nation through whom blessings of life would be mediated to others. For the Priestly Writer that promise is a continuation of the blessing imparted to all mankind "to be fruitful and multiply and fill the earth" (Gen. 9:1; cf. 1:28). In Genesis 17 the promise is linked with the Abraham covenant and intensified in typical Priestly fashion by the addition of superlatives. Thus the promise of seed is formulated as, "I will multiply you *very very much*" (v. 2), "You will be the father of a *multitude* of nations" (vv. 4 and 5), "I will make you fruitful, *very very much*" (v. 6), "I will make *nations* of you" (v. 6), "she shall become the mother of *nations*" (v. 16), "I will make him fruitful and multiply him *very very much*" (v. 20). This promise is repeated in similar terms to Jacob (Gen. 28:3; 35:11; cf. 48:4).

This expectation of numerous seed is balanced by a promise pertaining to the possession of a land. The Yahwist explicitly connects this promise with the land of the Canaanites and binds this promise alone to a covenant with the patriarchs in Genesis (Gen. 15:18). The accent of the Yahwist seems to be on the future empire of David (Gen. 15:19–20). The Priestly Writer emphasizes certain religious dimensions to this promise and underscores the duration of Israel's life in the land. The land is first of all a "land of sojournings." Such a title may reflect an empathy with the Israelite sojourners in exile among whom the Priestly Writer was living, or the tension between promise and fulfillment which the patriarchs and their seed in captivity knew as they savored this covenant hope. But the land is also pronounced an "eternal possession" (Gen. 17:8). God's covenant decrees have enduring outcomes. Hence the purchase of the cave in Genesis 23 is the first crucial step in demonstrating that truth. That cave and its environs are obtained as "a possession for a burying place" (Gen. 23:20). The field is a sacred plot representing the entire land; the burial possession is a kind of "down payment" or earnest of the land as an "eternal possession." Hence the Priestly Writer carefully reports how each of the patriarchal figures is returned to this place for burial. In death they anticipate the possession of all the land; their bodies are joined to the sacred soil (Gen. 23:19; 25:7-11; 49:29-33; 50:12-13).

Three other versions of the Abraham covenant promises appear in the Priestly records of Genesis. These programmatic passages develop the primary covenant messages of Genesis 17 and relate them to the course of patriarchal history (Gen. 28:1-4; 35:9-12; 48:3-7). Each of these texts is given in full here to illustrate the obvious literary link with Genesis 17. The first of these is spoken when Isaac pronounces a blessing upon Jacob, prior to his departure for Paddan-aram:

Then Isaac called Jacob and *blessed him and commanded him,* "You shall not marry one of the Canaanite women. Arise, go to *Paddan-aram* to the house of Bethuel, your mother's father, and take as wife from there one of the daughters of Laban your mother's brother. *El Shaddai bless you, and make you fruitful and multiply you,* that you may become a company of peoples. May he give the blessing of Abraham *to you and your descendants with you* that you may take possession *of the land of your sojournings* which *Elohim* gave to Abraham" (Gen. 28:1-4).

In contrast to the Yahwist version, this Priestly account reports Isaac blessing his son knowingly and willingly. Here we meet none of the trickery and subterfuge found in the Yahwist story (Gen. 27). Nor do we discover Jacob fleeing to Laban in Haran because of the antagonism between Jacob and Esau arising over the blessing (Gen. 27:41-45). Rather, the Priestly Writer reports Isaac commanding his son to visit Paddan-aram (not Haran) to obtain a wife from the family of Bethuel. And Jacob dutifully obeys. Jacob is no longer the scoundrel of the Yahwist narrative, but a faithful son and heir (Gen. 28:7). Moreover, during his absence from Canaan, Jacob has the assurance of an eternal possession when he returns. He did not leave under a cloud as the Yahwist suggests. For the Priestly Writer the promised land remains an eternal possession even for these far from its borders. That testimony must have sounded loud and clear to the exiled Israelites in Babylon.

Upon Jacob's return from Paddan-aram Elohim appears to him a second time and repeats his basic covenant plan:

Elohim appeared to Jacob again when he came from *Paddan-aram* and blessed him. *And Elohim* said to him, "Your name is Jacob; no longer shall your name be called Jacob, but Israel shall be your name." So his name was called Israel. *And Elohim* said to him, "*I am El Shaddai, be fruitful and multiply*; a nation and *a company of nations* shall come from you and *kings* shall spring from you. The land that I gave to Abraham and Isaac I will give to you and· I will give the land *to your descendants after you*" (Gen. 35:9–12).

The Yahwist had portrayed Jacob's return from Haran in terms of his confrontation with Esau (Gen. 32:9–12). Prior to that encounter the angel of Yahweh takes on Jacob in a wrestling bout (Gen. 32:22–32) in the course of which Jacob is given a new name honoring his victory. As is typical of the Priestly record, Jacob's new name is simply announced by Elohim and adopted without any explanation of the circumstances (Gen. 35:10). As with the naming of the segments of creation, a divine word is spoken and the name exists as an important given in its own right.

The promise to Abraham, Isaac, and Jacob is also given to Joseph in Egypt:

And Jacob said to Joseph, "*El Shaddai* appeared to me at Luz in the land of Canaan, *and· blessed me and said* to me, 'Behold I *will make you fruitful and multiply you*, and I will make out of you *a company of peoples*, and will give this land to your descendants as *an eternal* possession'" (Gen. 48:3–4).

In this way the Priestly Writer traces the dual promise of extreme fruitfulness and future possession of Canaan through the lives of each of the patriarchs. The first of these promises is fulfilled during the Egyptian captivity. A formal introduction to the book of Exodus acclaims the significance of this fulfillment. The seventy children of Jacob symbolize a perfect fulfillment corresponding to the original number who propagate the earth from Noah's household (Gen. 10). That perfection is verbally expressed when the writer adds:

But the *seed* of Israel was *fruitful* and *swarmed* and *grew very very* strong, so that the land was *filled* with them (Exod. 1:7).

Thus the first stage of the covenant program is finalized when Israel experiences the blessing of vast progeny. The second stage of the covenant plan awaits divine action. That action seems to be delayed until the appointed time, however, even though the oppression of Israel has reached a critical point. In that crisis, finally, "Elohim *remembers* his covenant with Abraham, with Isaac and with Jacob" (Exod. 2:23–24).

76

THE COVENANT REMEMBERED IN EGYPT

"Remembering" means setting a previous promise in motion. By remembering "his covenant" Elohim initiates phase two of his redemptive plan for his people. Here, the Priestly Writer continues to stress the personal and eternal character of the covenant initiated by God. He will "confirm" that covenant by completing its agenda. His remembering of the Noah covenant was associated with an appropriate covenant sign, the rainbow. God saw that sign and preserved his own promised order. On this occasion it is the groans of his people that stir Elohim to remember his own commitment. The heart of his covenant vow was to be the God of Abraham and his progeny. "I will be *their God*," he had promised (Gen. 17:8). The corresponding half of the traditional covenant formula reads, "And they will be *my people*." But those words were never spoken to Abraham, and their absence from Genesis 17 may be deliberate. For they are expressly announced in Exodus 6 as the second stage of the Abraham covenant plan is launched and the sons of Abraham are welded into a people through the exodus experience.

Genesis 17:1–8 and Exodus 6:2–8 complement each other in several important ways. They represent two phases of the same covenant program as it has been formulated by the Priestly Writer. Exodus 6:2–8 initiates the fulfillment of those promises which would make Israel God's people and give them a land of their own. Through Moses, God announces an agenda that will inevitably lead to the exodus, Sinai, and wilderness experiences. The importance of this second covenant campaign is underscored by the disclosure of God's covenant name, YAHWEH. That name was reserved for this hour and for Moses, the man of this hour. The correlation between the pronouncements of Genesis 17:1–8 and Exodus 6:2–8 is reflected in the progression of the following table.

THE ABRAHAM COVENANT PLAN

Stage One: Genesis 17:1–8	Stage Two: Exodus 6:2–8
The Narrator's Introduction:	
Yahweh *appeared* to Abraham and said:	And *Elohim* said to Moses:
The Divine Self-Identification:	
"I AM EL SHADDAI; walk before me and be *perfect*." v.1	"I AM YAHWEH." v.1

77

Reference to the Former Identification:

"I *appeared* to Abraham and Isaac and Jacob as EL SHADDAI, but by the name YAHWEH I did not make myself known to them." v.3

The Covenant Promise to Abraham:

"I will make *my* covenant between me and you, and I will *multiply you very very much.*" v.2 (expanded in vv. 3–6)

(Already fulfilled: Exod. 1:7)

The Covenant Established with Abraham's Seed:

"And *I will establish my covenant* between me and you and your seed after you throughout their generations for an *eternal covenant.*" v.7a

"I also *established my covenant* with them. . . ." v.4a

The Covenant Relationship Announced

"So that I might be *a God to you and to your seed after you.*" v.7b

"I will take you for *my people,* and I will be *your God* and you will know that I am Yahweh your God who brought you out from under the burdens of the Egyptians." v.7

The Covenant Promise to Abraham's Seed:

"And I will give to you and to your seed after you, *the land of your sojournings, the land of Canaan,* for *an eternal possession.*" v.8

". . . to give them *the land of Canaan, the land* in which they sojourned as *sojourners.*" v.4b

The Covenant Remembered:

"Moreover I heard the groaning of the people of Israel, whom the Egyptians hold in bondage and *I have remembered* my covenant." v.5

Announcement of the Plan of Action for Stage Two:

Therefore, say to the sons of Israel: "I AM YAHWEH"

a. Exodus

"I will bring you out from under the burdens of the Egyptians. . . ." v.6

78

b. Election

"I will take you as my people. . . ." v.7a

c. Conquest

"And I will bring you to the land which I swore to give to Abraham, to Isaac and to Jacob. I will give it to you for a possession." v.8

Concluding Affirmation of Covenant Purpose:

"And I will be *their God.*" v.8b.   "And you shall know that I am Yahweh *your God.*" v.7b

"I AM YAHWEH." v.8b

The links between Genesis 17 and Exodus 6 require little comment. Structurally Exodus 6:2-8 is bounded by the threefold "I AM YAHWEH" (vv. 2, 6 and 8). The first of these announces the new name of God as Yahweh and the passing of the era when El Shaddai was the divine choice. In Exodus 6:6 that same formula "I AM YAHWEH" introduces the new program for fulfilling the second great promise to Abraham, the gift of the land. The third "I AM YAHWEH" provides a fitting finale for this plan. That name is the new symbol of the revealed covenant God. To know God through that name becomes the purpose of all the mighty deeds leading to the fulfillment of the divine promises. Thus we continue to meet the new Priestly expression, "you (they) shall know that I AM YAHWEH" (Exod. 6:6; 7:5; 14:4, 18; 16:6, 12; 29:46; 31:13).

THE STRUCTURING OF THE COVENANT RELATIONSHIP AT SINAI

The pattern of activities from Abraham to Sinai was one of promise and fulfillment, command and obedient response. Both God and his chosen men had shown themselves to be faithful. Suddenly a new element is introduced. As they approach Sinai God's people rebel by murmuring against Moses and Aaron (Exod. 16:1-3). The Priestly Writer sees the counteraction of God in terms of a new self-disclosure. As Elohim, God had made himself known through his powerful word in creation. His flood had dealt with all disorder and his covenant had reestablished order with nature. As El Shaddai he had revealed himself through his living promises to the patriarchs. As Yahweh he had promised a series of mighty acts designed to bring his people to Canaan. In Egypt

79

his miracles were proof of his good intent. Yet despite the mounting evidence of his power and presence, his people rebel. It is at this point that Yahweh announces a new mode of revelation designed to restore order to the covenant community and verify Yahweh's role in the exodus event:

So Moses and Aaron said to all the children of Israel: "At evening you will know that it was Yahweh who brought you out of the land of Egypt, and in the morning you will see the glory of YAHWEH (*Kabod Yahweh*), because he has heard your murmurings against Yahweh. For what are we that you should murmur against us?" (Exod. 16:6-7).

To provide a classic demonstration of Israel's rebellious change of mood, the Priestly Writer draws upon the manna and quail traditions, despite their location at a different point in the wilderness wanderings according to earlier writers (Num. 11:4-35). This uprising of Israel evokes the advent of the *kabod Yahweh*. This expression of the divine presence is a visible force for order in the community. The *kabod* comes mysteriously out of the wilderness. A cloud covers the *kabod* and yet the people can recognize the numinous fire deep within that cloud.

At Sinai the *kabod Yahweh* descends and its cloud covers the mountain for six days. On the seventh day Moses is summoned to enter the cloud for a special communication from his God. On this occasion the *kabod* is described as a consuming fire resting on top of the mountain. That fire can apparently only be seen through the filter of the enveloping cloud (Exod. 24:15b-18a). Regardless of the precise visible imagery which the Priestly Writer wishes to convey, the function of the *kabod* seems evident. It reveals Yahweh in all his mysterious and frightening power. At the same time his *kabod* become the centralizing force for discipline and communication among the sojourning Israelite people. This concept of a visible hovering *kabod* wrapped in a cloud covering is unique to the Priestly Writer in the Pentateuch. It differs markedly from the trailblazing pillar of cloud by day with its corresponding pillar of fire by night found in other sources. For the *kabod Yahweh* is cultically oriented and describes that mode of divine revelation appropriate in the tabernacle. Once the tabernacle has been completed the *kabod Yahweh* fills the tabernacle itself while the attendant cloud rests over the tentlike structure (Exod. 40:34-35).

The Priestly Writer reports the entire worship program for God's people as a direct communication from Yahweh to

Moses while hidden in the cloud of the *kabod* on Sinai. The program is an elaborate set of directions to establish a cult for the covenant people and to maintain order through that cult (Exod. 25:1–31:18). The Priestly Writer relates the execution of these divine directives in terms almost identical with their original pronouncement (Exod. 35:1–40:38). Within this catalog of cultic activities, however, the tie between cult and covenant is made explicit. The ark and the tent of meeting are the specific locations where Yahweh meets with his covenant community to organize its members. Through his priests Yahweh communicates and governs his people (Exod. 25:21–22; 29:38–46; Num. 7:89). The priesthood is the governing force and the mediating agency of God's word once the decrees of Sinai have been pronounced.

The ordering of the covenant community through the cult can be summarized by the term "sanctification." Covenant, cult, and *kabod* are integrated by means of this Priestly concept. When Yahweh comes to the tent of meeting to communicate he also comes to purify; when he is present as his *kabod* he sanctifies priest and cult; when he "dwells" in the midst of his people as the *kabod* Yahweh he is their God. Through his advent in cultic glory they know he is Yahweh, the God of the exodus. Thus the conclusion of the directives on daily burnt offerings is virtually a series of covenant promises bound to Yahweh's cultic presence:

It shall be a continual burnt offering throughout your generations at the door of the tent of meeting before Yahweh, where *I will meet with you* to speak with you.

There I will meet with the people of Israel and it shall be *sanctified* by my *kabod*.

I will *sanctify* the tent of meeting and the altar; Aaron also and his sons I will *sanctify* to serve me as priests.

And I will dwell among the people of Israel and *I will be their God* and they shall know that I am Yahweh their God who brought them forth out of the land of Egypt *that I might dwell among them.*

I AM YAHWEH, their God (Exod. 29:42–46).

Of special significance is the final purpose clause in this series of promises. The exodus event was preparatory to God's ultimate goal, namely, to "dwell" in the midst of Israel. The previous verse (v. 45) juxtaposed "dwelling" among the people with the formula of covenant relationship,

"I will be their God." Through this unique dwelling a special covenant context is established. That "dwelling" immediately implies the presence of the *kabod Yahweh* which descended to "dwell" on Sinai (Exod. 24:16), to sanctify the tent of meeting (Exod. 29:43) and to fill the tabernacle while the cloud of the *kabod* "dwelt" over the tent (Exod. 40:35).

While the new promises of Sinai are not expressly connected with the "establishing" of a new covenant, they clearly imply the creation of a new covenant order comparable to that revealed to Abraham.[5] God reveals a new dimension of himself in the *kabod Yahweh*, he offers a series of unconditional promises, one of which is his assurance of being Israel's God, and he establishes the cultic program for the new community with an eternal covenant sign, the Sabbath (Exod. 31:12–17). Those activities of God spell covenant in Priestly thought. The Sabbath is first of all a sign of Yahweh's cultic function as the one who sanctifies his people from generation to generation (Exod. 31:13). The Sabbath, however, is expressly called a covenant sign indicating an eternal decision or deed of Yahweh. In this case the Priestly Writer cites the divine activities of creation and the sanctified seventh day of rest as the corresponding divine guarantee of security. Cultic order is therefore secured by a sign grounded in cosmic order (Exod. 31:17). This covenant word makes the ordering process complete. All the signs, decrees, and structures Israel needs are provided in the master plan of God as he reveals his will from creation order to cultic order, from the seventh day of creation to the Sabbath day of Sinai.

From this point on the Priestly Writer is concerned with organizing and preserving the cultic order of the covenant community. The Priestly blocks of material in Leviticus and Numbers continue to highlight the commands of Moses and the presence of the *kabod* as agencies for such preservation. For example, the *kabod* makes a special appearance to validate the priesthood of Aaron and his sons (Lev. 9). After the tribes are organized for the wilderness journeys, the cloud of the *kabod* sets the pace and becomes the divine signal for marching or resting (Num. 9:15–23). The *kabod* reappears before the tent of meeting at times of crisis to give

5. Recent research has tended to confirm the belief that the Priestly Writer did think of the divine decrees of Sinai in a covenant context. For example, the term "testimony" in "ark of the testimony" (Exod. 25:22) seems to mean covenant in the Priestly Writing. See Hillers, *Covenant: The History of a Biblical Idea*, pp. 158–65.

authority and direction to Moses and Aaron (Num. 14:10, 26–38 and 20:2–9) or to instigate immediate punishment (Num. 16:10–24, 27a, 35; see also Num. 16:36–50). With the death of the great cultic heroes (Aaron in Num. 20:23–29 and Moses in Deut. 34:7–8) the era of the ideal cultic community organized at Sinai came to a conclusion. The people of God had been created in Abraham's loins, blessed with great seed, rescued from Egyptian bondage, organized into a cultic family at Sinai and sanctified by the presence of the divine *kabod*. The journey was over. The gift of Canaan as an eternal possession once promised to Abraham was now an imminent joy.

That memory would be meaningful to the Israelites at many points in their history, but if the deductions of scholars are correct, the message is directly pertinent to the Israelites late in the exilic period. The debate over whether the Priestly Writer organized his materials in the exile or later still continues.[6] Certainly the Sabbath and circumcision became crucial marks of Israelite identity during the exile. Like the patriarchs and the Israelites in the wilderness those in Babylonian exile were "sojourners" and travelers awaiting the possession of their land. In the face of the prophetic accusation that Israel had broken the Sinai covenant and forfeited her election as God's people, the Priestly Writer accents the eternal character of God's covenants. His promises to Abraham remain unconditional and eternal. They precede Sinai. They remain the ground for continuing hope. And circumcision is the unequivocal sign of that hope. Even the Sabbath sign goes back to the unchangeable order of creation. With these assurances the Israelites in exile could take fresh strength in the promise to Abraham that Canaan would be their eternal possession, despite exile, punishment, and humiliation.

The preceding application of literary critical techniques has uncovered two literary portraits which are at the same time theological works. The contours of these literary sources correspond to the outlines of the Yahwist and the Priestly materials recognized by most Old Testament scholars. The Yahwist seems to be the great narrative interpreter of the

6. Among recent important efforts to date the Priestly Code we should mention A. Kapelrud, "The Date of the Priestly Code," *Annual of the Swedish Theological Institute*, Vol. 3 (Leiden: Brill, 1964), pp. 58-64, and J. C. Vink, "The Date and Origin of the Priestly Code in the Old Testament," *Oudtestamentliche Studien*, Vol. 15 (1969): 8-144.

Davidic era while the Priestly Writer appears to have been a cultic systematician speaking to the needs of the Israelite exile in Babylon or later. These hypotheses are secondary, however, to the new insights into the diverse motifs, interpretations, thought progressions, theologies, and messages which are unveiled by the discipline of literary criticism as applied to the Pentateuch.

Glossary

CRITICAL—Operating with careful reasoned judgment based on close scrutiny of the subject in hand.

DEUTERONOMIST—That literary source of the Pentateuch found primarily in the book of Deuteronomy.

ELOHIST—An early literary source of the Pentateuch usually dated about the ninth century. The name derives from the word Elohim used to designate God throughout most of this source.

FORM CRITICISM—The study of the history and function of the forms in which traditions or messages are communicated.

LITERARY—Having to do with the process of creating and writing a document or portion thereof.

ORAL—Having to do with the handing down of information, beliefs, and forms by word of mouth.

PRIESTLY WRITING—The latest of the literary sources of the Pentateuch usually dated in the time of the exile. The name derives from a worship emphasis found throughout this source.

REDACTION CRITICISM—The study of how literary materials are organized, interpreted, and modified by an author or editor.

TRADITION—The process of handing down information, beliefs, and customs from one generation to another *and* the information, beliefs, and customs thus handed down.

YAHWIST—The earliest of the literary sources of the Pentateuch usually dated about the time of David. The name derives from the word Yahweh which predominates as the name for God in this source.

Annotated Bibliography

ALONSO-SCHOKEL, LUIS. *The Inspired Word: Scripture and Tradition in the Light of Language and Literature.* Translated by Francis Martin. New York: Herder & Herder, 1965. Alonso-Schokel considers the literary question at an aesthetic and hermeneutical level that falls outside the scope of our study. His understanding of the philosophy of language makes his study of major importance in future literary critical research.

BEYERLIN, WALTER. *Origins and History of the Oldest Sinaitic Traditions.* Translated by S. Rudmen. Oxford: Blackwell, 1961. This scholarly analysis of the Sinai traditions incorporated in the text of Exodus demonstrates the necessity of offering a complete literary critical analysis of each textual fragment of the text before any comprehensive tradition critical study can be made. Beyerlin's work is a major contribution in this area.

CARPENTER, J. E. *The Composition of the Hexateuch.* London: Longmans, Green and Co., 1902. Carpenter's work represents one of the most comprehensive attempts among non-German scholars at the turn of the century to apply historical and literary critical techniques to every unit of the Pentateuchal text. A complete listing of literary terms and phrases and their relative frequency in each of the proposed sources is appended. An elaborate theory of composition and literary growth is proposed in this significant volume.

EISSFELDT, OTTO. *The Old Testament: An Introduction.* Translated from the German by Peter Ackroyd. New York: Harper & Row, 1965. This monumental Old Testament introduction appeared in several German editions before being translated into English. This composition is a major exhibit of how literary and form critical techniques work together to gain a more complete analysis of the origins, growth, and composition of each of the biblical books. A comparable major introduction is that of Georg Fohrer. *Introduction to the Old Testament.* Initiated by Ernst Sellin. Translated from the German by David Green. Nashville: Abingdon Press, 1968.

FUNK, ROBERT. *Language, Hermeneutic and the Word of God.* New York: Harper & Row, 1966. While much of the material in this volume relates to New Testament interpretation, the principles of recent linguistic analysis and hermeneutical theory are integrated with an understanding of the literary critical process for all of Scripture.

KRAUS, HANS-JOACHIM. *Geschichte der historisch-kritischen Erforschung des Alten Testaments von der Reformation bis zur Gegenwart.* Neukirchen: Neukirchener Verlag, 1956. The most significant analysis of the history of the historical and literary critical

85

method from the Reformation era until the present. A fine treatment in English is that of Emil Kraeling. *The Old Testament Since the Reformation.* New York: Harper, 1955.

NOTH, MARTIN. *Überlieferungsgeschichte des Pentateuchs.* Stuttgart: W. Kohlhammer Verlag, 1948. This work has become a classic analysis of the development of the central Pentateuchal traditions. Meticulously wrought prolegomena provide a complete division of the Yahwist, Elohist, and Priestly sources of the Pentateuch. These divisions become a kind of standard listing with which scholars agree or which they modify for various reasons. His commentary on Exodus provides an excellent example of how his rigid critical work has exegetical value. *Exodus.* Translated by J. S. Bowden. Philadelphia: Westminster Press, 1962.

ROWLEY, H. H. *The Old Testament and Modern Study.* Oxford: Clarendon Press, 1951. This book offers a complete survey of the major developments in critical research from about 1920 to 1950. A similar popular summary treatment has been done by Herbert F. Hahn and brought up to date by Horace Hummel. *The Old Testament in Modern Research.* Rev. ed. Philadelphia: Fortress Press, 1970. U. Cassuto. *The Documentary Hypothesis.* Jerusalem: Magnes Press, 1961. This work, translated from the Hebrew edition of 1941, represents a typical example of the efforts by Jewish scholars to examine critically the source hypothesis. Conservative scholars have also challenged the hypothesis on theological grounds. A notable example of this group of writers is G. L. Archer. *A Survey of Old Testament Introduction.* Chicago: Moody Press, 1964.

VOLZ, P., and RUDOLPH, W. *Der Elohist als Erzähler: Ein Irrweg der Pentateuchkritik.* In Beihefte zur Zeitschrift fur die alttestamentliche Wissenschaft. Vol. 63, 1933. Here Volz proposed a serious modification of the accepted theory of four major literary sources in the Pentateuch, suggesting that the Elohist and Priestly Writer were primarily editors of the great Yahwist storywriter. Rudolph completed the work of Volz in a less radical form.

VON RAD, GERHARD. *Die Priesterschrift im Hexateuch.* Beitrage zur Wissenschaft vom Alten und Neuen Testament. Vierte folge. 1934. A significant effort to isolate and treat one major literary source of the Pentateuch, the Priestly Source of the Pentateuch, on its own terms. This book remains a standard work on the subject. The relationship between form critical theory and literary criticism can be seen in the great programmatic essay of von Rad entitled "Die formgeschichtliche Problem des Hexateuchs." This and other writings of von Rad now appear in *The Problem of the Hexateuch and Other Essays.* Translated from the German by E. W. T. Dicken. New York: McGraw-Hill, 1966.